JANE ROBERTS  T2-CRY-082

"Many people are in the same position I was in when I initiated the experiments listed in this book: They've had one brush with an experience that doesn't fit the official views of life, and they want to know more. These simple experiments will send each reader who tries them on an inner journey—basically an unpredictable, creative one—for no two consciousnesses are the same."

Enter, then, the psychic world of Jane Roberts as Seth comes seemingly from no-where to become her mentor and guide—and possibly yours.

Her experiences and experiments will help you to tap psychic powers you never dreamed you had. And they will add refreshing and rewarding new dimensions to your daily life.

THE COMING OF SETH
was originally published by
Frederick Fell Publishers, Inc.

THE COMING
OF SETH

(Original title: *How to Develop Your ESP Power*)

by Jane Roberts

PUBLISHED BY POCKET BOOKS NEW YORK

THE COMING OF SETH

Frederick Fell edition published 1966

POCKET BOOK edition published April, 1976

This POCKET BOOK edition includes every word contained in the original, higher-priced edition. It is printed from brand-new plates made from completely reset, clear, easy-to-read type.
POCKET BOOK editions are published by
POCKET BOOKS,
a division of Simon & Schuster, Inc.,
A GULF+WESTERN COMPANY
630 Fifth Avenue,
New York, N.Y. 10020.
Trademarks registered in the United States
and other countries.

Standard Book Number: 671-80415-4.
Library of Congress Catalog Card Number: 66-17331.

Printed in the U.S.A.

*This book is dedicated to
my husband, Robert F. Butts, Jr.,
for his invaluable assistance.*

CONTENTS

Introduction

Writing a new introduction to this book sends me traveling backward ten years in known earth-time to the early days of my psychic explorations. More than that, though, I'm carried swiftly back and forth between the past and present lands of my psyche: I began speaking for Seth in a "mediumistic capacity" as I was writing this book, and in a way all the books that Seth and I have written since emerged from these pages.

The book was originally titled *How to Develop Your ESP Power,* and it was based on a series of experiments I devised as a result of my first sudden involuntary out-of-body experience. Here in these chapters I wrote the day-by-day story of those initial experiments that led to the coming of Seth. Each chapter contains excerpts from those early sessions. Seth came seemingly from nowhere. For all I knew, he would disappear back into the unexplainable, remaining only as a remembered psychological puzzle, a strange high point in my life, and I would return to my normal writing—enriched, but relatively unchanged.

The first publisher I sent the book to rejected it because of Seth's emergence, but offered to publish it if I deleted that part of the story. I was honest enough to refuse. It seemed all right back then to write about psychic phenomena if you investigated it and collected case histories about other people's experiences, but didn't cloud the issue by having any of your own—*that,* it seemed, made you less capable—as if you could explain an orgasm better and more scientifically if you'd never had one yourself. I felt that to be a curious attitude, and to a large extent it still prevails.

In any case, the book was published, but it "went no-where." I'd quit my job at an art gallery to finish it. The day it appeared in print, I started teaching nursery school. My husband, Robert Butts, and I were invited to appear on a New York television show. We backed out at the last moment after discovering that we were to be treated like psychic superspooks, expected to put on a great show with the "Ouija" board at the expense of our integrity and the audience's. We decided that we'd just keep up with our own sessions and let it go at that.

I wrote another book, on dreams and out-of-body experiences, in which I mentioned Seth almost as a foot-note, emphasizing the history of psychic phenomena and playing down my own growing experiences. Luckily the editor I sent the book to saw what I was doing and asked for a manuscript about Seth. This developed into the Seth Material.

But this first little book, as no place else, carries the initial enthusiasm in each page, the growing excitement, the countering intellectual questioning, the back-and-forth tension between the validity of our psychic experience and our need to explain it rationally.

There were few reviews for the book, but I was cautioned in some of them against leading my readers astray by encouraging experimentation with the "Ouija" board—which, some said, could lead to psychotic troubles at best, or possession by evil spirits at worst. And here again I maintain, ten years later, that evil spirits just don't exist in those terms; only the "evil" of superstitious fears, ignorance and dogmas that teach people to fear what they don't understand; the same kind of dogmas that lead people into fanaticism rather than tolerance, fear rather than courage, dependence rather than self-reliance.

Many people are in the same position I was in when I initiated the experiments listed in this book: they've had one brush with an experience that doesn't fit the official views of life, and they want to know more. They don't want to be saddled with the paraphernalia of someone else's dogma. They'd just like an idea of how to proceed.

And embarking upon such a search can be fascinating, daring, and amusing all at once.

For example, Rob and I were embarrassed to use the Ouija board the first time . . . and the second time . . . and the tenth time. It just seemed like a silly thing for adults to do. But children's games can strike adults as silly—precisely because they are so simple and direct, unimposing and imposing at the same time. If the "Ouija" board is "spooky" on occasion, it's because our love of scary excitement rouses—the unknown is at our fingertips —and if the "Ouija" board tells some bizarre stories, so do children's tales. Yet, once you learn to decipher the "language," you discover that the psyche sometimes needs to shake us out of the everyday to make its points.

In many ways this is a naïve book. I was unaware of most so-called psychic literature when I wrote it; and now I think luckily so, because everything, including the phenomenon of speaking in trance, was new to me. I didn't even know that it had ever been done before. Some of the questions asked seem oddly simple now; others, we're still in the process of answering. Yet ultimately it seems that answers to the most important questions only lead to more meaningful questions in which terms like "yes" or "no," "true" or "false," "real" or "unreal" finally vanish in a greater context of experience large enough to contain the incongruities, eccentricities and seeming contradictions in which our greater reality happens.

This book also marked an end and a beginning for me. As I wrote down my new experiences, old questions from my youth challenged my adulthood and led me to turn aside from my goal of a comfortable writing career in what is loosely called The Establishment. No longer could I clothe my intuitive knowledge safely in fiction. It was confronting me as a practical daily reality. There would be no fantasy novel about a "personality" called Seth, as in the past I'd written down my dreams as science fiction, hiding them behind conventional ideas of creativity.

That creativity had escaped "safe bounds." These experiments, listed here, worked—far more successfully than I could have imagined. I was astonished and a bit unsettled. It was perfectly respectable to use telepathy and clairvoyance as hypotheses for science fiction—no one was saying that we could really "read" minds, for God's sake. But suddenly these hypotheses jumped the fence of "maybe" out into the living room, and presenting such odd theories as known fact was something else again. "Occult literature" wasn't "in." Gone, it seemed, were my young hopes for recognition or good reviews from *The Saturday Review* or *The New York Times* book section. I didn't even consider nonfiction writing back then, but reporting—quite a different thing.

So my world, and Rob's, was shaken up to a considerable extent. At a neighborhood party to celebrate the publication of this book, I read some of my poetry and said nothing about the subject matter of the book at all, so ambiguous were my feelings. So *The Coming of Seth* marked my initiation into a new kind of reality, and I began my efforts to relate that greater world to the generally accepted one.

We'd had approximately two hundred Seth sessions when this book was finished. Now there are well over one thousand. Seth's own books, dictated while I was in trance, were still in the future, and at the time I would have been opposed to a "Seth book." Speaking for an "energy essence personality" Seth was one thing, but writing I considered my territory. How my ideas of the self have changed since! Now my territory has expanded to include many different kinds of experience then not acceptable as a part of my selfhood—or selfhood in general.

Then, I took every precaution possible in an ordinary living framework to be objective, to stand apart from my own psychic experiences, examining them with a polite but definite skepticism. Nothing wrong in that, and in the beginning of such ventures it's sound enough mental practice. But I referred to Rob in our hypnotic experiments as "the subject"; it sounded more scientific. Now I find it amusing: forget that this was a young woman hypnotizing her husband—leave out the emotional elements surely present in order to give the whole affair a more respectable air.

In examining human personality, scientists often try to bring down its characteristics to the manageable, to leave out the deeper elements that no electroencephalogram can ever decipher. So, sometimes, to some extent I tried to put Seth "out there" someplace, forgetting that whatever he is happens in and through my psyche.

But the arena of human experience and exploration can no longer be confined, even officially, to the exterior conditions of our environment. We have our being in an even vaster interior environment in which the psyche's emotional reality is every bit as "objective" as any physical object.

Actually, this is the first book of a continuing saga—something else we couldn't have known, at least consciously, when the book was written. The experiments listed here are simple and rudimentary, yet they certainly did work for us, and they will to one extent or another for each reader. We began with the "Ouija" board. It's the most preliminary method of activating the other portions of the psyche, a method that is considered quite unrespectable and disreputable by most parapsychologists. And certainly the results can be unwieldly, riotous, exuberant and "unscientific," as any highly creative material can be.

But this is not a book for scientists. It is a manual for ordinary people whose only access to a laboratory is their willingness to open the doors to the laboratory of the private mind. How does our consciousness work? How wide is its scope? Ultimately the answers lie in the unofficial as well as the official levels of our experience. These simple experiments will send each reader who tries them on an inner journey—and, basically, an unpredictable, creative one—for no two consciousnesses are the same.

Again, when I began this book I started out "from scratch." Yet Rob and I are constantly astonished, looking back, to discover that Seth's later detailed theories were all couched within those early sessions. His ideas concerning probabilities, simultaneous time, and moment points, among others, appeared publicly first in these pages.

This book is dedicated to Rob, and rightly so. It's because of his dedication and industry that the Seth sessions were faithfully recorded from the beginning, and it was his encouragement and understanding that helped me continue with these explorations. Rob and I embarked on this odyssey together, with no idea where it would end. We still don't know that, yet we've encountered new aspects of reality and tried to apply them to the world of daily experience.

Jane Roberts
September 1975

THE COMING
OF SETH

CHAPTER 1

How to Use a Ouija® Talking Board Set.
What Makes the Board Work?
We Meet Seth.

In the summer of 1913, a housewife in St. Louis got out a "Ouija" board as part of a parlor game. The pointer began spelling out a message from a female personality calling herself Patience Worth, who supposedly lived in England in the seventeenth century. Over a period of twenty-five years, Patience Worth dictated poetry and novels which were published and received critical notice. The housewife, Mrs. Pearl Curren, was not an educated woman. Her personality was nothing like Patience Worth's.

Patience wrote in the idiom of a bygone era, with authentic archaic spelling. She spoke casually in her fiction of daily household articles that have long since vanished from use and memory. The case was well investigated. No hint of fraud was ever discovered. Disagreements arise only from the various explanations given as to the origin of the Patience Worth personality.

Was Patience Worth the spirit of a woman long dead? Did she have significant knowledge of the seventeenth century because she had lived in it? Or had Mrs. Curren, unknown to herself, accumulated a fantastic amount of information, subconsciously, all of it pertaining to the past? If so, what was the source of the knowledge?

Many of the details given in the "Ouija" board messages were known only to scholars. If Mrs. Curren's sub-

conscious mind somehow picked up this wealth of knowledge, then this is evidence that the subconscious has at its
command abilities of which the conscious mind is unaware. Even this explanation for the Patience Worth case
leaves many questions unanswered. The sort of information given was not of the kind that is available ordinarily.
Where did it come from? How did Mrs. Curren's subconscious mind organize the material into novels and
plays?

On the other hand, if Patience Worth was actually a
personality who once operated within physical matter,
then a different set of questions present themselves. Did
she communicate through Mrs. Curren's subconscious
mind? Did she operate the "Ouija" board, or did Mrs.
Curren? In either case we are left with the fact that the
human personality is less limited by time and space than
we suppose.

I mention this case because the "Ouija" board played
such a part in the emergence of the Patience Worth personality. The board has been variously considered as a
method of releasing the subconscious, a means of communications between living and dead, and as a silly parlor
game indulged in only by the bored and neurotic. The
part played by the "Ouija" board in the Patience Worth
case was provocative enough, however, to convince me
that it deserved a place within any ESP investigation.

Neither my husband nor myself had ever seen a
"Ouija" board, but we obtained one. This chapter will
be concerned with our own experiments with it, their results, and complete instructions so that you can discover
exactly how to use the board for yourself.

The "Ouija" board itself is approximately 22 inches
long and 15 inches wide. On it, the letters of the alphabet are printed in two rows of large, easy-to-read capital
letters. The word "yes" appears in the upper left-hand
corner, and the word "no" in the upper right-hand corner.
Beneath the alphabet are the numbers, from 1 through 9,
plus a zero. At the very bottom of the board the word
"goodby" is printed in somewhat smaller letters.

A small pointer comes with the board. This pointer is

like a three-legged miniature table of triangular form. To operate the board, participants place their hands on the pointer. The pointer itself rests on the board. To acquaint yourself with the procedure, place your hands on the pointer and run it gently across the board. When the board is working properly, the pointer will move seemingly by itself, with no effort on your part at all.

"Ouija" boards can be purchased at many hobby shops. They are advertised in *Fate Magazine.* They can also be ordered from Parker Brothers, Inc., Salem, Mass., now the registered owner of the "Ouija" trademark. Boards are inexpensive and with ordinary care will last for many years.

You may have success with the board immediately. If not, do not be concerned. Our first attempts were disappointing. There was either no movement of the little pointer at all, or the letters that it indicated added up to gibberish. My own attitude at the time was a poor one. I considered that the "Ouija" board was beneath my serious concern. Intellectually I realized that it deserved a place in my investigations, but emotionally I was embarrassed and ill at ease. Obviously this is no attitude to have when you try the board, or anything else, for the first time. Our first efforts were so inept that I wonder even more at our later success.

Here are some steps for you to follow in your own initial experiments. Place the "Ouija" board so that it rests between you and your partner. Let the board take the place of a table so that one end rests on your knees, and the other end rests on the knees of the other participant. Keep your eyes open. There is no need to close them. Rest both of your hands on the small pointer, which you have placed on the board. Have your partner do the same.

Relax. When the board begins working, the little pointer will begin to move, indicating the letters which will spell out the message. If the board does not give results in the first few sessions of, say, twenty minutes each, do not be discouraged. With most of you, however, the board will work the first time. If it does not work right away, then perhaps your attitude is wrong. Try the board then in a lighthearted manner, in the spirit of fun. Remember, if we had given up in disgust after our first failures, the Seth Material might never have developed. This book might never have been written.

If questions are asked of the board, it is better if they be asked by one person at a time in the beginning. If the pointer does not move, repeat the question. Speak in simple sentences. You may whisper, speak aloud, or merely form the words mentally. Ask one question at a time. Make sure that you allow the board a sufficient interval in which to reply.

Exert very little pressure on the pointer. It cannot move if you press down too heavily upon it. If you feel strange at the board, open the session immediately with a question. A standard opening question is: Is there anybody there? Then, your following questions will naturally be affected by the replies given by the board.

If a message claims to originate with another personality, then ask questions that will give you the greatest possible amount of information. If the personality claims to be other than a living one, ask for the place and time of birth and of death. Later you may want to check up on details that you receive. Ask for the names of other members of the personality's family. Are they alive or dead? If alive, where do they live? If dead, when and where did they die? If a question is not answered, or the pointer seems to hesitate, drop the question for a while, and then return to it.

Some people find that the question-and-answer procedure inhibits them, or the board. If this is the case with you, then simply sit quietly with your hands on the pointer. Within a short time the pointer will spell out its own message, without any query from you. Later when you feel more at ease, you may use a combination of procedures, with excellent results. It is necessary that complete integrity be used by anyone working with the board. Distrust of a partner will seriously impede any progress you might achieve.

Experimenting with the "Ouija" board is a fascinating

experience, and perhaps the easiest way to begin any ESP experiments. I suggest that you try the experiments in this book in the order in which they are given, since one will prepare you for the next. The field of psychic phenomena is one of the few in which it is possible for the amateur to make contributions. It is important, therefore, that you take careful notes in all these experiments.

When working with the board, you or your partner may write down all questions and answers, either when the pointer halts between messages or when it just pauses, as it sometimes does. For efficiency, however, questions and answers should be written down by a third person when this is possible. Begin your notes with your very first session. Include the date, the names of the persons participating, and the time. If questions are asked, write them down and leave room for the answer to be inserted. When you are more familiar with the board, it is a good idea to plan questions ahead of time.

When the "Ouija" board is working well, you may have to devise some sort of personal shorthand since the messages will come so quickly. Ordinarily the board will not indicate punctuation, so you must watch to see where one sentence ends and another begins. Words may be run together, so that at first glance the message seems to be meaningless. For this reason, examine all messages carefully. In some cases, the board will use a shorthand of its own. The number 4 might be used for the word *for*. The letter "u" might appear in place of the word *you*.

In the beginning you may ask simple questions that can be answered by yes or no. Until you gain confidence, you may ask for initials instead of full names. Do not be overly gullible in accepting garbled messages. Do not try to make sense of nonsense by stretching your imagination too far. The board will spell out complete words, and then sentences, and you will also improve with practice.

Is is possible that a message that seems incoherent might be a legitimate communication in a foreign language, but this is not likely. Usually if you cannot make sense out of a message, there is none in it. File it away and disregard it, but do not throw it away. Later, in another chapter, we will discuss the ways in which you can evaluate such messages, whether they are received through the "Ouija" board or through other methods.

Do not be concerned if some aspects of your messages seem to contradict themselves, particularly in the beginning. These may be distortions of valid information. More will also be said on this subject later on in the book. By the third or fourth session you should be getting complete sentences, if you haven't already. After a month's experience with the board, Robert and I were receiving material that added up to ten typewritten pages per session.

It is quite an experience to feel the pointer move, and know that you or your partner are not consciously moving it yourselves. When we began our own experiments with the board, we didn't know what to expect. I'll give you a brief account of our early sessions, so that you will have something against which to measure your own results.

After our first two unsuccessful attempts, we began to get coherent messages that claimed to originate with my grandfather, Joseph Adolph Burdo, who died in 1949. Grandfather was French and Indian. He spoke English quite well, but with certain definite peculiarities. For example, he always pronounced the words *these, them,* and *those,* as "dees," "dem," and "dos." The board used his spelling, and the words in general were chosen with his characteristic manner of using the English language as a whole.

We also received messages that claimed to originate with other personalities who had survived death, personalities whom neither of us had ever known. We did check up on the birth dates and death dates as they appeared within the messages themselves. The material was consistent as a rule. The life histories given were certainly plausible. Up to this point we were both rather surprised, but not particularly impressed. For one thing, we could never get the same "people" back again when we tried the board the next time. We were, however, interested enough to continue.

After two or three such sessions, we were again besieged with gibberish. In the middle of nonsense words one clear phrase appeared: "eastern roads." Actually these words were significant, though we didn't know it at the time. We did, however, dutifully include the phrase in our records. This is one of the reasons why note-taking is so important. Sometimes a seemingly meaningless phrase may make sense later on, as this one did.

Our next "Ouija" board experiment marked the beginning of a unique experience that is still continuing. It began, inconsequentially enough, with a message from a personality I will call Frank Withers, though that is not the name given to us by the board. Frank Withers told us that he had taught English in Elmira, New York, for thirty years, and added other information concerning his background and family.

The next day I asked an older woman, a native Elmiran, if she had ever known anyone with the name given to us by the board. She stated emphatically that she had known of such a person and added that he had moved on the outer circle of her own acquaintances and had died in the early 1940's. Frank Withers had given the date 1942 as his year of death, a fact that the woman, of course, could not have known.

Our next few sessions continued in the same vein, with Frank Withers. For several reasons we didn't check further on this early material at the time. There were some obvious contradictions in dates, for one thing. For another, especially in the beginning, it was difficult to imagine that the information was legitimate in the usual sense of the word. Certainly the press of time had something to do with our negligence here (both of us had jobs), and also the fear of possible embarrassment in checking public records. We had no idea, then, that the "Ouija" board sessions were going to continue or that they would eventually develop into something else. We were merely pleased that we were able to experience a phenomenon of which we had only read in the past.

As it turned out, we were concerned only briefly with Frank Withers, for three board sessions. The next session opened with Frank Withers, but his personality was replaced by the Seth personality. The Seth Sessions had begun. It was immediately apparent that the board's messages had suddenly increased in scope and quality. We found ourselves dealing with a personality who was of superior intelligence, a personality with a distinctive humor, one who always displayed outstanding psychological insight and knowledge that was certainly beyond our own conscious abilities.

With this session the board began to spell out paragraph after paragraph, one after the other. Somewhat to my own dismay, Seth insisted early in the sessions that reincarnation was not only a possibility but a fact of human existence. He began listing previous reincarnations for Robert and myself, giving names, dates, family relationships and other details. Some of this material checked out through hypnosis. Other details are still to be checked. When sufficient material is collected, we will check all details against existing records. This will be discussed in the chapters on reincarnation.

Both Robert and I were familiar with the theory of reincarnation, but had discounted it for any practical purposes because of flaws that we considered insurmountable. To me, reincarnation smacked of the occult. Seth countered each of my protests with flawless logic and later listed experiments which could be used to prove the validity of the theory.

Was I moving the board? Was Robert? We began testing each other. I'd lift my hand off the pointer without warning. The pointer stopped. Rob did the same. The pointer stopped. Usually the board would not work for one of us alone. Both of us seemed necessary, but neither of us alone was moving the pointer.

Our first introduction to Frank Withers came on December 2, 1963. In our earlier sessions, we had never been able to maintain any consistency between one sitting and another. When the Seth sessions began, one session instantly began to reinforce earlier ones. Seth specified that we have sessions twice a week, naming the evenings and the time. Sessions varied from two to three hours each. Sometimes they are longer. We have followed this schedule ever since, and sessions still continue.

One phrase caught our attention soon after the introduction of the Seth personality. It occurred as Seth discussed Robert's previous reincarnations. According to Seth, Robert was a landowner in Denmark in the 1600's, maintaining farms near a city called Triev, which no longer exists. The words "eastern roads" were used to designate the location in Denmark, and we recalled the same phrase appearing in the middle of gibberish in an early session.

At the end of this chapter you will find excerpts from our early sessions. The questions we asked will help you form your own. Notice the earlier one-word board responses and the longer replies achieved by the fourth session. In all probability, your own experience will show this sort of progression.

But what makes the "Ouija" board work? Before I answer this, let us take a good look at the make-up of the human personality, for it is a part of this personality that allows this sort of communication to take place.

The ego is that part of yourself with which you are familiar in daily life. It is your conscious *I*. This conscious *I* is not a concrete thing. It is ever changing. It is not the same now as it was when you were a child, and it will not be the same thing tomorrow as it is today.

The ego is that part of you that faces the daily world and deals with practical problems. It is formed around certain abilities and inclinations that are part of your personality. Some of these are used and accepted by the ego, to become part of the conscious *I*. These likes and dislikes, abilities and characteristics which you consider your own, help compose the ego.

The ego is extremely important in everyday living. It enables us to concentrate on the practical matters at hand. Outside stimuli reach our brains constantly, however, and the conscious ego cannot handle this barrage of stimuli by itself. It is necessary that many be consciously ignored. We can only be aware of so many things at once. We perform many acts without knowing consciously how we do them. The ego is not even aware of many stimuli that originate within the body itself.

We walk across a room, change chairs, and pick up a book, for example. All the while we are engaged in these activities, we are, of course, inhaling and exhaling. Our physical cells are replenishing themselves. Yet consciously we are not aware of willing ourselves to breathe. We are not even aware of the muscular motions necessary for us to move from one chair to another. Not only that, but we have little conscious control over these activities. It is almost as if another self takes care of certain functions for us—functions that are very important to our physical survival—such as breathing and digestion. If they are not carried out with precision and excellence, we will die.

If so many aspects of vital nature are controlled by subconscious forces, in this case by the autonomic nervous system, is it so hard to believe that other functions and abilities are also controlled at a subconscious level? Hardly. Often we hum under our breath without being aware that we are doing so, for example. In sleep many of us walk around the room, sometimes out of the house and down the street, while the conscious mind is blissfully unaware of our activities. Indeed a sleepwalker's delicate balance can be disturbed if he is too quickly aroused or awakened.

A conscious interference with subconscious action, therefore, can disturb its smooth results. If we had to will each breath we took, consciously supervise the millions of small bodily manipulations necessary for daily locomotion, we would have no time for anything else. Nor, for that matter, is there any reason to suppose that we could better our present subconscious performance.

The "Ouija" board is, among other things, a method of reaching and communicating with this personal subconscious, this inner self that is so important to your physical survival. The personal subconscious knows more about you than you do. When the conscious *I* is relaxed, then the subconscious can express itself through muscular motions, as for example when you doodle on a piece of paper while speaking on the telephone. Your doodles are clues to this inner self. While your conscious mind is taken up with other matters, the subconscious is controlling your muscular motions, causing your fingers to scribble. The scribbles may seem meaningless to you, consciously, but in all probability they have definite meanings to your subconscious mind. Since many of our muscular motions are always controlled subconsciously, then it is not surprising that this inner part of ourselves can express itself through such movements.

It is believed that these same subconscious muscular motions move the little pointer across the "Ouija" board. If this were all, then the board would still be a most rewarding way for the conscious *I* to discover the hidden areas of the whole self. But it is my contention that this personal portion of the subconscious is but the topmost level of a more vast subconscious region. The Seth Material maintains that Freud's discovery of the subconscious represents only the first exploratory recognition of the whole inner self. Freud and Jung, according to Seth, only touched on the most obvious portions of what could be called "Undiscovered Man" or the "whole self."

But the subconscious contains more than inhibited primitive drives that must be held in leash by the individual and by society. It is also the origin of mankind's finest intuitions and perhaps the basis for language and civilization itself. It is very possible that a study of the layers of the subconscious can lead us to a knowledge of man's past mental and psychic existence, in the same way that a study of earth's physical layers gives evidence of past civilizations to archeologists.

As you follow the experiments listed in this book, you will discover for yourself that beyond this personal subconscious there is a reality as vivid and valid as any with which you are now familiar. The "Ouija" board will allow you to relax your conscious mind so that you can become aware, perhaps for the first time, of messages from this inner self. You will discover your own subconscious

our own personal subconscious areas, but you
o find that this subconscious is a threshold to
another inner reality.

Remember in your "Ouija" board experiments that the
key word is relaxation. Make sure that you keep neat, careful notes of each session. Write down the questions that
you ask as well as the answers you receive. The following
are excerpts from our own early sessions.

Although we had three earlier experiences with the
board, two that were successful and one with passages
that claimed to originate with my grandfather and other
personalities, we consider those preliminary and begin
our formal records with Frank Withers. The excerpt
then is from Session 1, in which Frank Withers made his
appearance.

Questions are in ordinary type. All board replies are in
large type, for your reading convenience. No changes
have been made. Answers are exactly as given, except
that the names have been changed to save possible
embarrassment to living persons. All questions were asked
by Robert F. Butts.

Excerpts from Session 1, December 2, 1963

Q. Is there anyone there?
A. Yes

Q. Will you give us your initials?
A. F W

Q. Please spell out your first name.
A. Frank

Q. Please spell out your last name.
A. Withers

Q. Can you give us the year of your death?
A. 1942

Q. Did you know either of us?
A. No

Q. Were you married?
A. Yes

Q. Is your wife alive or dead?
A. Dead

Q. In what year did she die?
A. 1954

Q. What was her first name?
A. Ursula

Q. What was her last name?
A. Alteri

Q. What was her nationality?
A. Italian

Q. What was your nationality?
A. English

Q. What was your profession?
A. Teacher

Q. What subjects did you teach?
A. English

Q. In what city or town?
A. Elmira

Q. How many years did you teach?
A. 34

Q. In what year were you born?
A. 1885

The following are excerpts from the second session. By now we were very curious, since this was the first time that we had the chance to resume with a contact made through the board.

Q. Are you there, Frank Withers
A. Yes

Q. Where did you spend most of your life?
A. Elmira

Q. Where were you born? In what house?
A. State Street

Q. In Elmira?
A. No

Q. Well, in what state, then?
A. In the state of sorrow

This answer intrigued us. It was the first time that the board seemed to reinterpret our question and answer accordingly. Perhaps the board answer led Robert to ask the next question. In any case neither of us had ever considered reincarnation as anything more than a rather implausible idea, so we were rather taken aback by what followed:

Q. Have you lived other lives on earth?
A. Yes

Q. How many?
A. Three

Q. When did you live on earth the first time?
A. 6 century

As the session continued, Frank Withers said that he had been a soldier in Turkey during one life and insisted that he had known Robert and myself in the city of Triev, in Denmark, during another existence. Among other details mentioned was the statement that I had been a man at the time, and the son of my present husband. Dates and locations were given, though it was made clear that the city of Triev no longer exists.

The third session was much like the first two. The fourth session was a turning point, however. It marks the withdrawal of the Frank Withers personality and the introduction of Seth. The general tone and quality of the Seth sessions were immediately apparent. Discussions began here that were to become the basis for many future sessions.

Answers changed from the earlier one-word or one-sentence replies to full paragraphs, all spelled out by the pointer. The intelligence of the answers made the sessions more enjoyable. The personality of Seth took over, at once individualistic and definite. This session begins with Frank Withers, and ends with Seth.

Excerpts from Session 4

Q. Are you there, Frank Withers?
A. Yes

Q. Do you have a message for us?
A. Consciousness is like a flower with many petals.

Q. Is this Jane's subconscious talking?
A. Subconscious is a corridor. What differences does it make which door you travel through? Nevertheless I can speak through her if I so choose. Once she spoke through me. You cannot see the joke of course. Ha.

Q. When did you speak through Jane?

A. A century ago. Seance. She was a medium reaching me for you. I came through too.

Q. Frank Withers, can we refer back to you on any specific questions in the future?

A. Yes. I prefer not to be called Frank Withers. That personality was rather colorless.

Q. We need some kind of a name to use in talking to you.

A. You may call me whatever you choose. I call myself Seth. It fits the me of me, the personality most clearly approximating the whole self I am, or am trying to be. Joseph is your whole self more or less, the image of the sum of your various personalities in the past and future . . . You are Joseph, the Joseph you see in your mind, the blueprint.

Q. What would you call Jane, as you call me Joseph?

A. Ruburt

Q. Would you clear this up a bit?

A. What's to clear?

Q. It seems like a strange name to us. I don't believe Jane likes it.

A. Strange to the strange.

Excerpts from Session 6

Q. Isn't it true that we are more or less at the mercy of the subconscious?

A. Yes but that is like saying that the whole is at the mercy of its parts. Man just hasn't learned to use his parts effectively. The sum of all should be excellent consciousness. Individual consciousness is all important. It never loses but gains. Each time it expands to include more.

Q. Out of curiosity, Seth, what do you do between sessions?

A. What do you do?

Q. Can you give us more information concerning the name Ruburt?

A. That was Jane's name once long ago as yours was Joseph. Both represented high points for your entities, images in the mental genes, blueprints for the spirit to follow. Joseph and Ruburt represent the full scope of your earthly personalities, toward which you must grow. But in another sense you are already Joseph and Ruburt, since the blueprint exists. Everyone has such a blueprint. Through each life the individual tries to follow his. The pattern is not imposed, but is the entity's own outline.

Q. Doesn't this interfere with free will?

A. How? You made the blueprint yourself, and your various incarnated selves are not aware of the blueprint. They have free will. You gave it to them. That's the challenge.....

CHAPTER 2

Use the Ouija® Talking Board as a
  Stepping Stone.

I Speak for Seth—Experiments for You.

How to Test Your Own Results.

Voice Communication—Automatic Writing.

Can you imagine yourself speaking for hours at a time, intelligently and without hesitation, on such matters as the Nature of Physical Matter, the Subconscious, the God Concept, Anti-Matter or Time? Can you imagine yourself giving logical, even eloquent answers to such questions put to you at a moment's notice? Can you imagine such a situation taking place despite the fact that the words you speak are not your own, and consciously you do not know which word will follow another? Can you imagine carrying on such a performance at the end of a normal working day, and on a consistent basis?

Before I began the experiments for this book, such circumstances would have struck me as most unlikely. Yet, in little over a year I have dictated for Seth in a trance state over 2,000 pages of such material, clearly and concisely, with no contradictions and without any of the normal hesitations of ordinary speech. It is possible that some of you will find yourselves doing the same thing in your own way. If you have seriously tried the "Ouija" board experiments given in the last chapter, you may have already discovered for yourself that the board can be a stepping stone to something else. It is possible that you have already increased the scope of your own awareness.

Increasing awareness actually expands the self, in a literal manner. Consider for a moment: What are the real limitations of the self? Are you limited as a self? What boundaries separate you from everything that is not yourself? Skin would seem to be the divider between our physical selves and other physical objects. But skin not only separates us from the rest of the universe, it also connects us with the rest of the universe.

Much comes through our skin without which we could not exist. Everything that we know of in the universe is composed basically of the same ingredients. Except for a difference of molecular organization, we are composed of the same physical stuff as a table or a chair or a peach or a crab. Our skin differs from the seemingly empty space just outside it simply in degree and density.

Through the skin, which is itself alive, we receive nutrients from air and sunlight without which we could not survive. We eat portions of the universe in the form of fish and meat and plants, and make them part of ourselves. They are used by our bodies and then returned to the earth to be used again. Physically, then, the self is composed of all these alien unselflike elements. In other words, the physical self is not basically limited by the skin. We could just as easily say that the self is extended by the skin, out into the environment so that it can draw in nutrients.

You may insist now that the self, your self, is limited psychologically. You may insist that the self is definitely limited in some fashion, even though you may not be able to define the limitations. But now, consider your self again. You are your ideas, your thoughts and plans and emotions. Certainly. But these do not exist in a sort of mental vacuum. They are formed by your own heredity and environment. They are modified by people with whom you come in contact. In turn you modify the thoughts and emotions of others.

For convenience's sake, we humans act as if the physical self ended with the skin. We act as if the consciousness of ourselves was all enclosed inside our heads, with the skull like a bony fence that keeps our identity safely inside. But this is not the case. Certainly there is such a thing as identity, but no one has quite discovered exactly what it is. Some clues as to the real nature of identity will be given later in this book.

We are now becoming aware that telepathy exists. If we can pick up the thoughts of others and transmit our thoughts to others, then what happens to our old ideas about the limitations of the self? We will have to change our concepts considerably as ESP investigations prove them *passé*. The psychological self reaches much further than we have ever imagined.

Again, it is very possible that the subconscious as we now know it represents only a glimpse of the whole self. Beyond it may reach unchartered regions to which the self has access, regions that contain realities that we have done our best to ignore.

The ego, however, is not concerned with inner reality. It deals with everyday practical problems. It is comparatively rigid. Even though it changes constantly, it dislikes change. This was necessary in man's early evolutionary development. If the caveman was to survive, all his attention had to be focused intently on the physical environment. A daydream, a momentary journey into the subconscious self, could cost him his life. The ego developed and hardened with use into an armor-like shell that now threatens to bury the self that it was adopted to protect.

Experience with the "Ouija" board helps loosen this tight-fitting ego. It gives the inner self breathing room. Slowly, like some small animal waking from hibernation, the inner self can begin to waken. The personal subconscious is the first portion that is allowed some freedom. For one thing, it is the only part of the inner self with which we are usually familiar. For another thing, it is just beneath the ego, though only in a manner of speaking. There are no literal directions, such as upper and lower, to the self.

Experience with the "Ouija" board will help relax the personal subconscious, and these habits of relaxation will help you in other ways. Intuitions and impulses to which you have not listened in the past will make themselves known. You will feel as if you have been expanded or renewed. And so you have. Bit by bit you will become aware of realities that you previously ignored. You will be expanding the limitations of your self for all practical purposes, since you will be able to add to your own experience in a way that was not earlier possible.

You will discover that the subconscious does not end with your own personal buried memories. You will not hit bottom, find a dead end, reach the final limitations of yourself or your awareness. There will not be a point beyond which you cannot go if you want to. You will not reach a spot and feel, "I end here. Beyond this, my self stops."

As there is no roof to the sky as our ancestors believed, so there is no boundary, top or bottom, to the human personality or to your own awareness. Our rockets explore outer space. We can also journey into inner space. No one else can do it for us. No one else can do it for you. The venture is more than worth the while.

The area of the personal subconscious, first reached, may surprise you. It is neither a dungeon of dangerous impulses that must be repressed nor a utopia of natural goodness. It is a storehouse for all the impressions and abilities not accepted by the ego at any given time. It is the threshold between the so-called conscious self, and those vast inner areas of the self of which we know so little.

In your own explorations of this inner reality you will need to use common sense, intellectual honesty and self-discipline as well as the intuitional portions of your nature. You will need all your capabilities in order to evaluate your own experiences.

First I will explain the development of my own initiation into these realities and give you some ideas concerning the various experiences that may open up to you as a direct result of your "Ouija" board experiments. Continue with your sessions at the board. Many of our later experiments do not make use of the board at all, but you will gain by the practice in relaxation that it allows you to achieve.

In my own case the board led to what I call voice communication. It was entirely unplanned and unexpected. I had not even listed such phenomena in my original experiments. I can only tell you how to recognize voice communication if it happens, how to use it, and how to test the validity of your results.

With some of you, a proficiency for automatic writing instead of voice communication may show itself as a result of "Ouija" board experiments. This chapter will also include directions for automatic writing, though for various reasons my own abilities do not seem to lie in this direction.

As you continue with the board, some of you may find that you begin to anticipate the answers that it will give to your questions. This can happen in any session, the first or the twentieth. The development is determined by your own personality and abilities. It may never happen. If it does, it may be the first sign that you are gifted in a most rewarding area of extrasensory perception.

From our third "Ouija" board session on, I began to anticipate words, phrases, then complete sentences. I would know in whole or part what the board would reply to Robert's questions. I waited, somewhat reluctantly, while the pointer spelled out its replies, but I didn't trust my inner answers either. I suspected at the time that my personal subconscious was having a good time at my conscious expense.

As sessions continued, I became progressively uneasy. I began to pick up whole paragraphs before the pointer had completed one sentence. At the same time, I became annoyed with the slow board process. Robert had to pause, write down the questions he was going to ask, return his hands with mine to the pointer while the answer was spelled out, then pause again to write down the reply. This took considerable time.

Though the pointer spelled out the same message that I received mentally, I still distrusted the inner message on the one hand, and felt impelled to speak it aloud on the other. I did not hear a voice. Whole sentences simply sprang into my mind, seemingly from nowhere, but the words were not my own. My reluctance was obvious. Finally Robert asked the board: "Seth, why is Jane rather reserved about our contacts with you? I can tell that at times she isn't too enthusiastic."

Through the board Seth replied: "She is concerned because she receives my messages before they are spelled out. This would make you cautious, too."

On another occasion Seth remarked through the board: "Jane, you give your subconscious a lot of credit. Give credit where credit is due." I felt as if Seth were nudging me to speak the replies aloud. But rather than leap off into unknown depths, I clung to the "Ouija" board like a reluctant swimmer to dry shore.

For one thing, I feared failure. Seth was even then discussing subjects of which I know little. I was afraid of making a fool of myself, beginning a weighty message only to break off, hemming and hawing. Or suppose the messages drifted off into nothing? At the time I had only Seth's word for it that he wasn't a part of my own personal subconscious. I feared being swept away by psychological forces of which I knew little. My ego and I stood firm. I kept on receiving the inner messages, but I refused to dispense with the "Ouija" board. Nor did Seth push me, but the inner reception persistently continued. Matters remained at this stage until session 8. For five sessions, then, we had a stalemate.

Such reluctance is, indeed, the sign of a healthy ego. In all these endeavors we are not trying to ignore the ego. We are simply training it to become more flexible, so that it will allow the inner self more freedom. The ego is an important part of the personality, necessary for our relationship with physical reality. Through our experiments we will show it that it has nothing to lose and much to gain through allowing us this freedom. Such recognition will actually result in the expansion of the ego and in the expansion of the self in general.

For this reason, all the experiments in this book should be supplemented with a healthy outgoing attitude toward

other people and relationships. If you are already a with-
drawn, introspective person, you should make efforts to
relate yourself with others through outside activities. This
will ensure a balanced growth of your abilities, and the
gradual acceptance of your inner potentials by your
conscious mind. The ego will resent your inner explorations to some extent. Do not try to browbeat it into sub-
mission. The ego needs to exercise itself through outward
behavior. Do not allow your interest in ESP to deprive
the ego of any of its needs. We want a balanced acceptance of inner abilities by all portions of the self.

By our own eighth session, I was apparently convinced,
or my ego was convinced, that greater freedom could be
allowed. In the middle of this session I suddenly shoved
the "Ouija" board aside, stood up, and began to dictate.
My voice at the time was perfectly normal, though since
then definite voice changes have shown themselves. The
words I spoke, however, were definitely not my own.

From the ninth session to the thirteenth, we used the
board only to spell out the first messages, which I could
not receive mentally for a while. Almost instantly this
allowed us greater speed of communication, but at the
beginning of each sitting I still felt a momentary nervousness at the thought of "letting go." Now I am hardly ever
bothered by such feelings.

Almost immediately we realized that I was in a light
trance during this dictation. The method of delivery can
be called automatic speech or voice communication. My
own conscious thoughts recede, along with my consciousness of my surroundings. There is nothing compulsive
about this, however. At any time it is possible for me to
return to normal consciousness. No invasion is involved.

By the fourteenth session we no longer used the board
even for these first messages. Since Seth suggested it,
sessions have been held on certain designated evenings,
twice a week. For the first year I paced the room constantly while dictating, with my eyes wide open, but without any real consciousness of my physical surroundings.
Now I speak sitting down, with my eyes closed, and with
no real consciousness of my environment at all. Robert

takes a word-by-word handwritten record of each session, which he then types. We always have ordinary lights on in the room. Every half hour we have a rest period.

I am a fairly intelligent human being, and a good conversationalist, but by no stretch of the imagination could I speak consciously, without pause or backtracking or confusion, for hours at a time on any of the subjects covered in the Seth sessions. The material constantly unfolds. One session builds upon another. Seth, in our 150th session, for example, refers to points that he made back in the twelfth session, and elaborates upon them further. On several occasions I have spoken in a deep masculine-like voice, much unlike my own, and with astounding volume. Many of the sessions have been witnessed. Besides general material, the sessions have given us valuable information concerning our own personal lives and psychological insights that have been of great practical use in daily life.

Yet, I had no reason at all to suppose in the past that I had any such abilities. You may also have such undeveloped capabilities. The "Ouija" sessions will prepare you for the experience if it does occur. It is also possible that your talents may be in the line of automatic writing instead of voice communication. In other words, you may be able to write the message automatically. This has one definite advantage in that your notes are more or less taken for you. It takes Robert several hours each week to type out the Seth Material.

Therefore, in your "Ouija" sessions, have an extra large piece of paper or pad and a soft, dark pencil handy. If you begin to anticipate the board messages, you will know it. There is nothing more persistent than this inner reception of information. I felt as if I must speak the words. You may feel, instead, as if your fingers want to write the words down.

If this is the case, then place the paper over the board, or sit next to the board with a pad on your lap or on a table. Take the pencil in your hand and place it at the top of the page. Write your name and then wait. Soon the pencil will begin to move. The action itself will be caused by your own subconscious muscular motions. The letters may be poorly formed. If so, do not let this bother you. Here also a shorthand may be used, as with ordinary board messages. You may write "u" for the word *you,* for example. More will be said about subconscious shorthand of this kind later on in this book.

As your hand writes, you may actually do something else also, such as watch television or talk with your partner. Do not keep watching the piece of paper to see what is written there, as this may impede your progress. Automatic writing is not so unusual an occurrence as voice communication and it is possible that many of you may learn to write automatically without too much difficulty.

You may, of course, try automatic writing itself, without any "Ouija" board. In this case, simply suggest mentally that your subconscious mind will use your right hand to write on any subject that it desires. You may feel your fingers tingle slightly. Be relaxed. Divert your conscious mind by some other activity. Listen to music, for example. Two or three sessions of twenty minutes each should be enough to let you know whether or not automatic writing will be easy for you.

All of you will not have abilities along these particular lines. Some of you may not take the time necessary to achieve the inner flexibility necessary. Others will be surprised at the relative ease with which their capabilities will make themselves known. But everyone who reads this book will have success with many of the experiments.

A large number of readers will receive messages from the "Ouija" board. How can you determine their validity? How can you tell whether they are springing from your own personal subconscious or from other layers of perception that are part of a deeper reality?

Any such material, received through the board, through automatic writing, or voice communication, should be carefully studied. Generally speaking, if your messages claim to originate from famous dead personalities, you can discount them as valid information. In all probability they are creative fabrications of your own personal subconscious.

If your material claims that you were a renowned historical figure in a past reincarnation, such as George Washington or Joan of Arc, for example, this is probably wish-fulfillment on the part of the personal subconscious. This does not mean that you must discontinue, or that the messages should be discounted as worthless. They may be delightful fantasy, and you may be using your abilities of creative imagination for the first time in your adult life. Such material can tell you much about your own subconscious existence. It may be considered as creative fact but should not be mistaken for practical fact. Certainly don't expect your friends and relatives to give you special favors because your "Ouija" board messages claim that you were once a member of some royal family.

The above caution may sound far-fetched, but if you have not paid any attention to your subconscious, if you have been familiar only with your conscious self, then your first experience with your own inner self may seem almost magical. Some people will be tempted to take as fact the most exotic subconscious tales, so it is well to examine your material carefully. Communications from the personal subconscious can be most beneficial. This area of the self, governing inner biological functions among other things, has intimate knowledge of your physical health and also of abilities and knowledge that may be hidden. It is, however, with even deeper layers of the inner self that this book is mainly concerned.

In checking your own messages, ask yourself the following questions and answer them honestly: Does the material itself seem to satisfy any repressed needs? Through the material are you able to vent personal prejudices that you are usually restrained from expressing? Do you feel superior delivering the material? Is the material excessively emotional, particularly in religious or sexual expression? Does it display any evidence of hate?

If the answer to any of these questions is yes, then it is most probable that the material comes from your personal subconscious. If it displays prejudice, then you can be fairly certain that, underneath ordinary consciousness, this prejudice is your own. If the material is in any way overly emotional, then this may be a sign that you are repressing your emotions in daily life. The material can be most useful in showing you where your own abilities and liabilities lie. If the material is entertaining, creative, fictional, then perhaps you have creative inclinations that you have not used in the past. Such knowledge of yourself will allow you to use your talents.

If, however, the material displays superior psychological insights, intellectual abilities beyond your own, definite elements of clairvoyance or telepathy or other ESP phenomena, then by all means study it with particular care. You may have a strong psychic awareness. You may be reaching into realities of which we know relatively little.

Do not overestimate or underestimate your own messages, whether you receive them through the "Ouija" board, through automatic writing or voice communication. If the material is valid it will prove itself out through time, through its own quality and accumulation.

The Seth Material has been severely and objectively studied by Robert and myself, and it has gained, not lost, through such scrutiny. For several reasons we are now convinced that it does not originate with my subconscious, at least as the word is generally used. It does not spring from my personal subconscious. For one thing, we can discover no satisfactions or needs that are being satisfied in the sessions that are not satisfied in my daily life. For another thing, it seems that even the subconscious would grow tired of having sessions twice a week at specified times, sessions that last two or more hours. The subconscious does not usually work in such a well-ordered, disciplined fashion, even when conditioning is taken into consideration.

The subconscious explanation for the Seth Material would also be more convincing if it were not for certain definite effects that have been displayed during sessions. Evidence of telepathy and clairvoyance has been given during some sessions. Unusual physical effects have occurred also that will be discussed in later chapters of this book.

Psychologists often call personalities like Seth secondary personalities. Professional mediums call them controls. The designation given to such personalities does not change the nature of the personalities themselves, and does not aid us in understanding them. Seth says that he is not a control, as the word is generally used. He also insists that he is not a secondary personality. There is no invasion in our relationship. I do not feel controlled by someone else. My consent is necessary at all times. Sometimes I do feel as if my self has somehow expanded.

I am convinced that a study and comparison of such manuscripts might prove valuable, not only to psychologists and parapsychologists but to the world at large. The intellect deals with ideas, but we are not at all sure that ideas originate with the intellect. It is more than possible that ideas are outcroppings of the intuitive processes. Many of our valuable inventions and concepts have come "out of the blue," and only later have been put to practical use. Manuscripts of this kind might be found to contain similarities of information that is valid—information that is unknown to the thinking brain whose function it is to deal with physical problems.

It is true that such material comes through layers of the personal subconscious, even if it does not originate there, and must contain personal distortions. It is also true that the intellect makes its own kind of errors, and is not thought less of because of them. We take it for granted that the mind does not always work at its best, and make allowances automatically. The same kind of allowances should be made for the workings of the inner intuitions.

Again, if you find yourself anticipating your "Ouija" board replies, take your time. Dispense with the board when you feel confident in doing so. You may find that you alternate for a while between the board and automatic writing or voice communication. You may find it difficult at first, as I did, to just "start out." In this case, use the board to begin sessions, then switch to automatic writing or voice communication.

Continue to take careful notes of all sessions. It is much better to have one or two definite, scheduled sittings per week, than to have three or four enthusiastic sessions one week and none the next. If you find yourself alternating between the board and automatic writing or voice communication, then make sure that this fact is plain in your notes. You should be able to tell clearly from them which portions of the material were received from the "Ouija" board and which were not.

Relax. Trust your own abilities without being gullible. If you receive contradictory or inferior material, do not be discouraged, but continue. Save such messages but do not count them with much validity, and try again.

If, on the other hand, your communications show signs of definite superiority of content or quality, then scrutinize them carefully. If predictions are given, check them out whenever this is possible. All of the Seth predictions have proved to be valid, but we never would have known whether they were correct or not if we had not kept strict records, and then checked later events.

If you are writing automatically, do not be surprised if the writing is unlike your usual writing, if the words are arranged in a strange manner upon the page. The writing could even be backward, or go from left to right. The letters may be badly formed. The subconscious cannot be expected to express itself in the same manner as the conscious mind. Even material that comes from those deeper areas of the self, beneath the personal subconscious, has to pass through that personal layer.

If you find yourself using voice communication, do not be surprised if there are any voice changes, though they may or may not appear. If a change is noticed, if the voice does not sound like your own, make sure that the voice is clearly described in the notes. Include also the length of time the changes were apparent. On occasion I have used a voice that was loud, deep, more masculine than feminine. While this was startling the first time it happened, it did give the Seth personality a vividness that was unmistakable. My own vocal cords suffered no damage.

To end this chapter, I will give you some excerpts from session 12. This was received through voice communication, and is an example of the early material received in such manner. As I spoke for Seth, I paced the room constantly. My eyes were open but my consciousness of my environment was limited. The room was lit in ordinary fashion. There were none of the usual hesitations of ordinary speech. The session, a fairly normal one as far as time is involved, lasted from 9 until 11:15 P.M. For reading convenience, all such material will be in large type.

As far as fifth dimension is concerned, I have said that it is space. I will have to try to build up the image of a structure to help you understand, but then I must rip out the structure because there is none. Consider then a network of wires, a maze of interlocking wires endlessly constructed so that looking through them there would seem no beginning or end.

Your plane could be likened to a small position between four very spindly and thin wires, and my plane could be likened to a small portion in the neighboring wires on the other side. Yet not only are we on different sides of the same wires, but we are at the same time either above or below, according to your viewpoint.

If you consider the wires as forming cubes— this is for you, Joseph, with your love of images— then the cubes would also fit one within the other, without disturbing the inhabitants of either cube one iota, and these cubes are themselves cubes within cubes. I am speaking now only of the small particle of space taken up by your plane and mine.

Again, think merely in terms of your plane, bounded by its small spindly wires, and my plane on the other side. These have also boundless solidarity and depth, yet in the usual circumstances, to one side the other is transparent. You cannot see through, but the planes move through each other constantly. I hope you see what I have done here. I have initiated the idea of motion, for true transparency is not the ability to see through, but to move through. This is what I mean by fifth dimension.

Now, remove the structure of the wires and cubes. Things behave as if the cubes and wires were present, but these are only constructions necessary even to those on my plane, in order to make things comprehensible to our faculties. We construct images consistent with the senses we happen to have at any particular time. We merely construct imaginary lines to walk upon.

So real are the walls of your room that you would freeze in winter without them, yet there is no room and no walls. In like manner, the wires that we constructed are real to us, although there are no wires. All is one, as you are one with the apparent walls of your room. Again the idea of transparency. The walls are truly transparent to me, though I am not sure I would perform, dear Joseph and Ruburt, for a demonstration.

Nevertheless, to me the walls are transparent. So are the wires that we constructed to make our point about fifth dimension. For all practical purposes we behave as if the wires were actually there. Again, if you will, consider our maze of wires. I will ask you to imagine them filling up everything that is, with your plane and my plane like two small birdnests in the network of some gigantic tree. . . . At a later date I will go deeper into this discussion.

Consider, for example, that these wires are also mobile, constantly trembling, in that they not only carry the stuff of the universe but are themselves projections of this stuff, and you will see how difficult it is to explain. Nor can I blame you for growing tired, when after asking you to imagine this strange structure, I then insist that you tear it apart, for it is to be no more actually seen or touched than is the buzzing of a million invisible bees.

CHAPTER 3

A Do-It-Yourself Seance.

Our Experiments.

Experiments for You.

When I began this book I wanted to discover what chance the interested beginner had of using his own psychic abilities. I was convinced that these powers were latent in every individual and represented natural characteristics belonging to the race as a whole. I had never been to a seance. Neither had Robert. Our reading in the field of ESP led us to the conclusion that some seances at least might be legitimate demonstrations of certain aspects of extrasensory perception. Other seances of which we read seemed to be based on no more than fraud or overworked imagination.

We decided to try a seance of our own. As it happened, we tried our first do-it-yourself seance on the spur of the moment and I will report it here along with an experiment for you to try yourself. Later some definite physical effects have been seen during Seth sessions, but these will be dealt with in the later chapters of this book.

On the evening of this particular seance, our first, a friend, William Cameron Macdonell, stopped in at our apartment for a visit. He had read the transcripts of our first Seth sessions. At this time only ten sessions had been held. The three of us decided to try a seance that night.

It was a week past the Christmas holidays. I still had Christmas candles in the windows. They were electric, with red bulbs. We switched them on, and turned off the other lights in the living room. Outside, a street light shone directly into the adjoining kitchen, so we closed the curtains in both rooms. We sat down, holding hands, at a small table that is approximately twice the size of an ordinary typing table.

There was sufficient light in the room so that we could see clearly. Since we weren't sure exactly how to begin, Robert asked Seth to give us some kind of a sign. On Robert's direction, I took my ring off and put it in the center of the table. We clasped hands, keeping them far away from the ring. Our hands were visible to us at all times.

Before beginning, we had closed the green café curtains so that we would not get reflections from the white blinds and candles. Then we concentrated on the ring. Within a very short time it began to glow and twinkle. We bent closer. The effect was definite—so was the cause. Robert found that by moving his arm back and forth, he could make the twinkle appear and disappear. The light was caused by reflection, despite our efforts to preclude such effects. We broke off and placed the electric candles behind the curtains and the blinds, where the light was diffused. Then we went back to the table.

This time Robert suggested that I place my hand, palm up, in the center of the table. I did so. Again Robert asked for some kind of a sign. My hand was clearly visible against the dark table covering. My other hand was tightly clasped in Robert's, on the table. Suddenly I spoke the words: "Watch the hand." One part of my mind wondered why I had spoken, but another part was self-assured. I repeated the words, speaking for Seth.

As we all waited, I felt the hand, my left one in the center of the table, grow cold. Before our eyes the hand began to change shape. It took on a definite pawlike form, thickened considerably below the thumb to the wrist, and seemed to grow in volume. Through me Seth asked if we saw the transformation clearly. It was obvious to all three of us.

The hand was palm up on the table. But suddenly the hand had nails on the opposite tips of the fingers, and the fingers at first appeared to be bent backward in a manner that no fingers could possibly bend. Yet my hand felt no strain. We bent closer to get a better look, and saw that there was actually a second set of fingers above my own. The rest of my hand retained its strange thick shape, seeming to expand or bloat as the fingertips glowed so that we could clearly see what was happening.

Then the extra set of fingers disappeared. One moment they were clearly visible; we all got a good glimpse of them. The next moment they were gone. Now the whole hand was fat and thick. I am a small woman with hands to match, except that my own fingers are fairly long. Now however the fingers were short and stubby. Through me, Seth said: "The hand is now Frank Withers' hand. Frank Withers had fat hands . . . he was a fathead." The humor in his voice (or mine) was apparent. In other early sessions Seth displayed amused tolerance when mentioning Frank Withers, although according to his own testimony, Frank was a part of Seth's own personality.

During the seance I spoke in my usual tone of voice more or less, except that the words were not my own. All the while that my hand continued its transformation, Seth commented on the phenomenon, mentioning that he was doing much better than he thought he could, for a first try. The hand still retained its thick shape, with the shortened fingers and fat form. Then Seth suggested that I put my right hand beside the strange left one, so that the two hands could be compared. He seemed anxious that we examine the effects, so as to be sure of them. I put my hands close together. The difference in them was no illusion.

Then I placed my right hand back in Robert's hand, and kept my left one in the middle of the table. Seth suggested that Robert now touch this odd stubby hand of mine. Robert did so, somewhat gingerly. The hand was different in texture, and wet. Though Robert felt the fingers and knew that they were there, the hand changed back into a pawlike appendage that he could see very clearly, and the appendage had finger stubs rather than regular fingers. What really impressed us, however, was a small detail. Before the hand had merely seemed fat. Now it grew in volume, up from the table, growing in thickness.

Yet Seth wasn't finished. When all hands were joined again, except for my changed left one, the hand began to rise from the table, although my arm and wrist remained right where they were. Bill Macdonell quickly passed his own hand between the rising one and the tabletop to make sure that this wasn't some kind of illusion. All the time my wrist was pressed tightly against the table. We checked this at the time. As the hand rose, it glowed slightly so that we could see it better. Then it returned to the table. Seth severed connection, and we took a break.

We were all tired but intrigued. We had begun at 7 P.M. It was now after eight. We decided to return to the table. Again, Robert asked Seth for a sign. I placed my left hand in the center of the table and put my right hand in Robert's. This time almost immediately my left thumb turned white, not just whiter than the rest of my hand but a whiter-than-chalk white that glowed. As we watched, the whiteness spread up from the thumb to the mound beneath it and crept up my arm midway to my pushed-up sweater sleeve. The lower portion of the hand grew thick again, seeming to grow up from the hand itself like a growth of some sort. This was by far the most startling of the effects, especially since a minute before my palm had been filled with shadow. Now the shadow completely disappeared, and the palm of the hand filled in with white, and kept growing brighter. There was no reflection at all to cause such an effect. The whiteness was of such intensity that it was unmistakable.

Bill Macdonell had seen several apparitions in his lifetime. Earlier he had asked us to question Seth about a large cloaked figure that had appeared by his bedside one night. Without being asked, Seth now volunteered the statement through me that Bill was part of an entity called Mark, and had twice been a man and once a woman. The apparition had been a past personality fragment that had materialized to warn him against high places. At one time, according to Seth, Bill in a previous life had taken to the trees at nightfall to escape animals. He had been hunting.

Here Seth broke off and began to laugh. "He escaped the animals, but fell asleep in the tree, fell out, landed on his head and was killed. He should avoid high places. He died at 46." Seth continued to say that Bill had trouble with balance. His rather macabre humor was startling, coming right after the chalk-white changes in the hand. Bill, incidentally, had been painting houses and using ladders during the time of the apparition. He is an art teacher by profession.

Again Seth broke contact. We were exhausted, but decided to see if Seth could materialize a full-length figure of some kind in a doorway that leads to the bathroom. We arranged the table in front of the open doorway and sat down. I felt Seth at once. He was annoyed. "This isn't a lunch session," he said through me. (Robert was finishing a piece of candy that he'd picked up during the short break.) "Nor is it a circus session," Seth said. He then added that too much light came through the bathroom window and suggested that we close the door.

On the back of the door, facing the living room, is a full-length mirror. Through me Seth told us to arrange our table and chairs so that we could all see our images clearly in this mirror. We did so. Then he told us to watch my image in the mirror. I sat with Robert on one side of me and Bill on the other.

I wore a black sweater all that evening, and my hair is short and black. The black hair and black sweater served to frame my face and neck. When we first looked into the mirror, my image was as clear as Robert's or Bill's, no more or no less. The electric candles were still lit. We were in semidarkness, but again, there was enough light to see objects. Our images in the mirror looked commonplace enough. Our hands were in clear sight on the table.

Everything else in the mirror remained the same except for my image. It did not change at once, but gradually the head grew thinner. The neck became squat, and even the hair changed its arrangement, molding the head in a much tighter manner. The head now looked more like a man's than a woman's. The shoulders became distinctly distorted, sharper, and more hunched. The contours of the face continued to lengthen. The image lowered its head. This was very startling to me, as I was looking up, straight ahead into the mirror.

A set of features appeared in front of the mirror image and seemed to move forward from the mirror, hanging out in front of it. The features glowed twice and then disappeared. At the same time Robert saw an aura about the head of the mirror image. Seth volunteered that the aura was part of the astral body, and that the image itself was part of another entity. I was very tired. The whole thing seemed to drain my energy. My head slumped down on the table. Our first attempt at a seance was over.

Our reactions to the evening were mixed. Earlier, before the experiment, we were rather embarrassed. Then we were intent and intrigued, though cautious. After it was over, we suspected some suggestion played a part in the mirror image; however, we couldn't be certain. The hand episode was fascinating, and we were positive that suggestion had little to do with this. The effects were too definite, and we checked them in several ways. The hand had without doubt changed shape, volume, and color. Extra fingers had appeared with the nails opposite to the nails of my own fingers. The hand had risen from the table although my wrist was pressed to the tabletop. Bill had checked this. The white glow that filled the palm and rose up to the arm was also unmistakable.

The scrutiny that we gave to the various manifestations of the hand were far too careful to be carried on as if all three of us were merely under suggestible influences. We were wide awake, curious. We did not accept everything that we saw. The first twinkle of the ring, for example, we quickly realized came from the reflections. Though I spoke for Seth, my eyes were wide open.

Physical effects of which we are more certain have

shown themselves, though not often, in the Seth sessions. We feel more certain of them simply because they happened while the room was fully lit and while no attempt was made to bring them about. But there is no question in our minds that definite effects did occur in this seance session.

If you have an open mind and a healthy intellectual curiosity and are relatively free of superstition, then you will find that an experimental seance of your own can be most interesting. If you do receive any definite physical effects, then you will discover for yourself that seances can be more than fraud or gullibility. Keep an objective frame of mind. Check whatever you see. On the other hand you must allow your intuitive self some freedom or there will be nothing to check. If you are absolutely positive that nothing will happen, in all probability nothing will. If you are curious and open-minded then you will not be bound by preconceived ideas of what is possible and what is not possible, but you will be objective enough to study any materializations soberly and reasonably.

These results were received on our first try. We had no such experiences before. We did not know much more about seances than any of you who read this book. There is no need to be afraid of "ghosts" or "spirits" or to approach this sort of seance as something unnatural. We are attempting to study on a logical basis many matters that have long been hidden in superstition. If materializations take place, then it is simply an indication that we do not understand what nature itself is. We do not understand the potentials of the human personality.

For centuries we have known that mind influences matter, but we have not known how. At the end of this chapter I will include some excerpts from the Seth Material which begin to deal with such questions. According to the theory presented in the material, every individual forms physical matter on a subconscious basis, including the physical matter of the personal image. As we are not consciously aware of our own digestive processes, so we are not consciously aware of the ways in which we constantly transform energy into physical matter. If this is the case, then human personality is basically free of physical laws as we know them. There would be nothing unnatural, then, in the survival of the personality, and nothing unnatural if such a personality once again formed a physical image and appeared to us in the form of an apparition.

Later we will discuss such matters more thoroughly, for your own experiments with dreams and telepathy will show you that the personality—your personality—is more independent of space and time than you suppose. Now, however, here are a few suggestions for a do-it-yourself seance. Our own later experience suggests that darkness or near darkness is not necessary at all. For your first attempt you may have the room dimly lit if you prefer. Perhaps semidarkness will allow you greater inner freedom at the start. You may feel embarrassed or silly with the lights on. Later, however, use normal lighting. You will be more certain of your results.

If you have the room dimly lit for your first attempt, make sure that you eliminate any sources of light reflections, by experimenting with several arrangements. Take time to arrange your table and chairs. They should be placed so that you can see clearly. Cover the table with a dark, opaque material to offset the possibility of reflections. Make sure that all persons present have their hands in sight at all times. It is a good idea to hold hands. You will never trust your results if someone's hand was not visible. Any number of persons can participate. These should be people whose integrity is beyond question. Check all effects that you see.

You may just sit quietly without speaking if you prefer. Or you may ask, "Is there anyone here?" You may appoint someone else to ask the questions, if you feel uncomfortable doing so yourself. It is much better if a person sitting at the table, but not participating, takes notes. If nothing happens within a period of a half hour, end the experiment and try another time. In the beginning particularly you may need several such attempts before you are relaxed enough to get any results.

If by chance someone in the group begins to use voice communication or speaks words that do not seem to be his own, then question him gently. Do not startle him. If any of the persons participating are overly suggestible and seem uneasy, then end the experiment. Such experiments are entirely safe with ordinary people. Undertaken with common sense and curiosity, they can be most instructive. Some people will go overboard in almost any situation, and these people should not be invited to participate in your experiment. They are too excitable to report objectively on any results you may achieve, and their very over-suggestibility may cause you to doubt what may be valid effects.

If voice communication results, ask questions as suggested in the last chapter, and examine such results according to the same rules given previously. I recommend that you not touch anyone who is using voice communication. He may be in a light trance state. This is a quite natural psychological condition, but a touch could cause disorientation. Such a person could become startled or uneasy, and the contact could be lost.

The following excerpts from the Seth Material are very interesting. As far as I know this is an original explanation of the ways in which mind and matter interact. Seth himself does not seem interested in producing physical effects. His preoccupation seems to lie with explaining ESP phenomena in general—what it is, how it works, what laboratory experiments can prove its validity. The following excerpts are from a session that is basic to any understanding of the subject matter discussed in the Seth Material.

Obviously it is impossible to include more than a small fraction of the Seth Material in this book, but Seth goes into the specific ways in which each individual subconsciously forms his own physical image, his environment, and the physical universe. He explains how the appearance of durability, width, height, weight, and placement in space are agreed upon and maintained. In the chapter The Spirit World: Does Matter Matter? these ideas will be discussed briefly.

From the Seth Material

Creation constantly continues, and not always along the lines of old patterns. On your own plane there is a subconscious storehouse of knowledge whereby it is known by all molecules and atoms exactly which evolutionary attempts have been made, and with what results, always with an eye out for circumstances that might fit forms once attempted with failure.

All atoms and molecules have a condensed consciousness; so do even smaller particles. The atoms and molecules that make up all physical matter and cells are not basically bound by your time. They act within the framework of your time, but the condensed knowledge that they contain carries with it its own peculiar and unique consciousness, that is not bound by physical laws.

Chemicals themselves will simply not give rise to consciousness or life. Your scientists will have to face the fact that consciousness comes first and evolves its own form. The physical body that you imagine consists of some sort of separate consciousness, controlling a framework of completely unconscious parts, is quite far-fetched.

All the cells of the body are individual and have a separate consciousness. There is a gradation here, but every cell is a conscious cell. There is conscious cooperation between the cells of all the physical organs [of the body] and between all the organs themselves.

Here is a case in point. The molecules and atoms and smaller particles all contain separate consciousness. Now, they form into cells. Although the cells maintain individuality and do not lose any of their abilities, there is actually a pooling of individual consciousness of atoms and molecules to form an individual cellular consciousness. . . . You end up with organs composed of literally unnumbered individual cells. This goes on ad infinitum, and even the lowest particles retain their own individuality. The cooperative nature of the physical body could be no mere result of your chemicals and chemical reactions.

Thus consciousness forms its own materialization. The physical body is a more wondrous phenomenon than is supposed, for this combination of consciousness continues and its results can be seen in the human brain.

When the physical origin of your universe is finally discovered, your scientists will be no better off than they are now. They will be up against the problem that they have avoided for so long, that of origin behind origin. The physical universe and everything in it is the result of consciousness. It did not evolve consciousness. To the contrary, consciousness not only created the physical universe but continues to do so.

The constant creation of the physical universe is carried on by each individual, on a subconscious level, through the use of mechanisms which I have at least partially explained. This constant creation of matter is not maintained through some localized subconscious that exists somewhere between two ears, behind the forehead. The individual subconscious is the result of a psychic pooling of resources and abilities. It is a *Gestalt*, maintained and formed by the cooperating, generalized consciousness of each atom and molecule of which the physical body is composed.

Each individual atom has the capacity, to some degree, to construct its portion of energy into physical construction. The whole physical structure of the body is the result of this cooperation of cells [which all contain their individual consciousness]. The pattern of the physical body makes it possible for all the cells, atoms and molecules to express themselves. They share in the perspectives reached through the abilities of a physically large body structure in a way that they could not otherwise.

As the various cells maintain their individuality, so also do the various personalities retain their individuality and uniqueness, while still cooperating to form the psychic structure of the entity, which in one context also forms them: and with this little problem I will let you take your rest break. There are more ways to see what is inside an egg than by cracking it, as you will discover . . .

Nor is man alone in maintaining the physical universe, in giving it continuity as he projects and constructs his own physical image. As this physical image is the direct result of his own inner psychic climate, as it faithfully reflects his own joys and illness, as these joys and illnesses show in the physical image, so do all living things construct their own images and help maintain the physical properties of your universe.

CHAPTER 4

Precognitive Dreams.

How to Remember Your Dreams.

Do You Have Precognitive Dreams?

Find Out for Yourself.

Do you have dreams that foretell the future? Your first answer may be a surprised, "No, of course not." You may amend the statement by adding, "At least if I do have such dreams, I never remember them." It is my contention, however, that all of us have dreams that give us a preview of future events, but that these dreams are usually forgotten.

Valuable knowledge is thereby denied to us. It is very possible that in your own dreams you receive a glimpse into the future, of which your waking self is unaware. This knowledge is not forever beyond your reach, however. There are methods of bringing it into consciousness, and the experiments listed in this chapter will allow you to achieve considerable results along these lines.

A precognitive dream is one in which you receive valid information concerning the future. A precognitive dream can be clairvoyant, as when you foresee a future event. A dream can also be clairvoyant but not precognitive, as when you see in your dreams an event separated from you in space, but happening at the same time as your perception of it.

As a rule, three factors are necessary before precognitive dreams can be considered at all airtight in scientific terms. The dream must be told to another person or persons as soon after its occurrence as possible. There must be reliable evidence that what the dreamer actually saw in his dream did occur later in the physical world. It must be shown that this information could not have been received through normally accepted sense perceptions.

If all these conditions sound discouraging, let me hasten to remind you that, despite them, many thousands of precognitive dreams have been documented and collected by recognized psychic societies. First-hand accounts of precognitive dreams from your own trusted friends and relatives, however, will probably do more to convince you of the validity of such dreams.

I suggest that you begin questioning your own acquaintances, family and friends. You will discover that people are anxious to talk about precognitive dreams, and this private investigation will serve to open your own eyes to the fact that such dreams are not as unusual as you might at first suppose. You must understand, however, that unless the dreams have been carefully written down, no scientific validity can be given to them. For your own benefit, apply the three factors mentioned above to all cases of precognitive dreams which are told to you.

My husband and I are pleased to include among our friends Mr. Ernfred Anderson, internationally known sculptor. Mr. Anderson told me the following dream. On a Saturday night in 1918 he dreamed that he saw his young sister dead in a casket. The sister lived in Sweden, and Mr. Anderson lived in New York City. As far as he knew, his sister was in good health. She was twenty-two years old, a mother with a young baby. On the next night, Sunday, he told his dream to the ten or twelve persons present at a party at his home. On Monday he received a telegram informing him that his sister had died on Saturday night, the night of his dream.

Years later Mr. Anderson met his dead sister's daughter. Now a young woman, she told him that the family often spoke of the fact that her dying mother's words were addressed to her distant brother in New York—Ernfred Anderson. In this case, Mr. Anderson received specific information, the knowledge of his sister's death. He told the dream to the people at the party before he received the telegram that informed him of her death.

This sort of dream is almost always remembered. The emotional content is so vivid and disturbing that a strong impression is made and even the conscious mind is aware of the data received. But what about more insignificant everyday events? Do dreams give a glimpse into more mundane aspects of reality? My own experience leads me to answer yes. Often, however, these dreams are not retained by the consciousness because the events foreseen are as unexciting as the actual events themselves. But how can any legitimate glimpse into the future really be considered unexciting?

Such dreams may occur more frequently than the more startling variety, but they may fit so smoothly into our habitual patterns of activity that we do not give them any attention at all, unless the event foreseen in the dream actually happens within a very brief span of time. For example, another friend, Dorothea Piry Masters, dreamed the exact amount of a bonus expected by her husband. The amount was so large and so out of line that she told the dream to her husband. Two weeks later when the bonus actually arrived, it was in the same amount foreseen in the dream.

A neighbor of ours dreamed that she and her husband would look at a house on Westmount Avenue in Elmira. The couple had been house-hunting, so she thought nothing about it, though she did mention the dream to her husband. She forgot the dream until the end of the week when a real estate man called, asking her to look at a house on Westmount Avenue.

This neighbor's husband then proceeded to tell me of a recurring dream of a nature completely unfamiliar to me. He dreams of seating arrangements which then work out faithfully in every detail. For instance, he dreamed that certain friends visited, and took definite places on the couches and chairs. The friends did visit and as he watched, rather dazed, they took the exact seats as those they had taken in his dream. He also dreams of such arrangements during the holidays. When friends and relatives sit down for dinner, they take the same seating arrangements as he has foreseen. He told me of these dreams in an embarrassed manner. Unfortunately he had not told his wife of these experiences, and kept no records.

One night Robert had the following dream. He saw himself driving three passengers down a snowy hill. It was storming badly, and road conditions were poor. In the dream he commented upon the dangerous situation to the other passengers. A car ahead didn't make it around a curve, and crashed.

Robert wrote down his dream and told me about it. We laughed, saying that the dream could hardly be clairvoyant, since it was April and the weather had been lovely. Four days later, at Easter, we entertained Robert's parents for dinner. In the middle of the afternoon a sudden snowstorm developed. Within a few hours, snow had piled up everywhere. We decided to drive the older people home, to a distant town. We did so, then had to return ourselves. The road conditions were precisely those of the dream. As we rounded a curve, we saw that the car ahead of us had gone off the road. Robert had been commenting about the inadvisability of driving in such a storm.

Dorothea Piry Masters told me another dream. She saw herself in this dream reading a slip of paper, a bank notice informing her that she was overdrawn to the amount of $3.61. In the morning she remembered the dream and looked at her checkbook. It showed a balance of $44.00. Since she had business at the bank that day, she asked the clerk to check her account. The clerk did so, then handed her a slip of paper containing the information that her account was overdrawn to the amount of $3.61. It is very possible that this dream originated with the personal subconscious, but regardless of its origin it contained quite practical data.

The following dream of my own is also interesting. It concerned an elderly neighbor of mine. She stood in a black suit on the staircase in the lobby of a hospital. To the left was a staircase, to the right was a partially enclosed gift shop where presents could be purchased, presumably for the patients. My neighbor was crying. Her eyes were extremely red and sore. She told me only that she was going away and didn't want to go. I told the dream to my husband in the morning, and wrote it down. Later that day I ran into my friend. With tears in her eyes she told me she had just learned she must go to the hospital to have an eye operation.

Robert and I had just returned from a Maine vacation. We had not corresponded with our neighbor, nor seen her since our return the day before the dream. Later when she was taken to the hospital, severely ill, I went to visit her. I had never been inside the hospital, but there to the right in the lobby was the identical gift shop I had seen in my dream.

Again, this dream made a strong impression upon me because of the emotional content, but less emotional dreams are often forgotten. When Mr. Anderson told me the dream concerning his dead sister, for example, he also mentioned in passing a dream he had the night before in which he discussed the artist Picasso with a friend of his. I was working in an art gallery at the time and Mr. Anderson had come into my office initially to discuss a Goya print which his friend had given to him only that morning. I stopped Mr. Anderson and asked if the Goya print belonged to the same man of whom he had dreamed.

Bewildered, he said yes. He had never realized the connection. The print had been given to him the morning after he had dreamed of his friend in connection with Picasso. Taking into account that distortion of some kind confused the names of the artists, Picasso and Goya, this dream is still interesting.

But what about you, the reader? Often a glimmering of such dreams remains with you in the instant you awaken, and then disappears. If the foreseen events happen within a few days, you may remember the dream. Otherwise it is forgotten. In most cases you simply forget most of your dreams to begin with. My first experiment for you is designed to help you remember your dreams, and to recognize whatever information they contain. This eximent was used by J. W. Dunne in 1927, and by various other investigators in later years.

An acquaintance was convinced that he never dreamed at all. He could never remember having a dream. Now this is an extreme example of the powers of the conscious mind to inhibit subconscious data. My acquaintance promised to follow the experiment which I will outline for you. Within three weeks he divested himself of a misconception that he had carried for years. He now is able to remember his dreams. The experience has been rewarding and beneficial to him. Before I began this experiment I recalled very few dreams. In the next chapter we will see how we can train ourselves in such a way that these sleeping activities are retained to an even greater degree.

Now for the experiment itself. Each night before retiring, place a notebook and pencil either under your pillow or on a small bedside table. Before going to sleep tell yourself firmly that you will remember your dreams on awakening, and write them down immediately. These instructions should be given several times when you are relaxed and ready to doze off. Within a week's time you will find yourself recalling large segments of your dreams. The proportion of dreams that you remember will increase as you continue with this practice.

As you write the dreams down you may find that you recall more details than you did when you first awoke. Do not be discouraged, however, if the first few days bring no results. What is involved here is the setting up of a new habit. This takes some time and effort, but the results are more than worth your while. If necessary, set the alarm clock ahead five minutes, so that you have time enough to record the dreams without rushing.

More self-discipline is needed here than may be at first apparent. The instructions must be followed exactly. In the morning, lie with your eyes still closed. The dreams will still be in your memory. Write them down at once. Do not get out of bed. Do not have a cup of coffee first. As you write down your first remembered dream, you may recall others. Date your dreams. This is extremely important. Write down those details that are in your mind, but make sure that you do not consciously add to your dreams.

This is only half of the experiment. Using this procedure, you will be able to recall your dreams, but the second half of the experiment will enable you to check dream events against reality; that is, to check dream events against events as they occur later in physical reality. The second half of the experiment will give you conscious knowledge of your own abilities to perceive future events in dreams.

Refer often to the notebook in which your dreams are written. Compare the day's activities with the dreams of the previous few days, or the previous week. Even though you have written your dreams down, you will forget them if you do not read them over to refresh your memory. Reading my own notebook, for example, I am astonished to find that many dreams are almost unfamiliar. Consciously I have forgotten them, even though I have recorded them.

Check the notebook carefully. If you dream of an event in which a friend or relative is involved, write at once or make some attempt to check. You can do this without mentioning your dream if you choose. This constant checking is necessary, and fullest benefits can only be achieved by following through in this manner. Here is a case of my own in which such checking was important, although I was tempted not to bother.

I dreamed that my brother-in-law's sister-in-law walked with me down a street. She had just lost a baby and had left the hospital moments before. I asked her what her husband was thinking of, to leave her alone at such a time. That was the end of the dream.

To begin with, the young woman lived out of town. I had met her only two or three times, many years ago. I didn't know her well enough to write her and ask if she had recently lost a child. Nevertheless, I wrote the dream down and dated it. A few months later, my brother-in-law came to visit us. His wife is the young woman's sister. Casually I asked him how his sister-in-law was. He told me that she was fine, although she had suffered a miscarriage not long ago. I murmured regrets and mentioned that her husband must have found the situation difficult also. Then my brother-in-law told me that the woman's husband had not been with her at the hospital.

If I had not written the dream down, dated it, and made an effort to check the dream events against actual events, I would not have known that the dream contained valid information. Incidentally, I have never dreamed of this woman before or since. The time of the miscarriage corresponded roughly to the time of my dream. My brother-in-law was not certain as to the exact date of the woman's miscarriage, but the time of the month was correct.

Again, it is necessary that you date each dream. When a dream event actually does take place in the everyday world, then make certain that you write this fact down under the dream notation, in a space left clear for this purpose. Also write down the date and any other pertinent information. The dating is particularly important since you want to know for certain that the event happened after, not before, the dream involved.

How can we accept the fact that some dreams are precognitive? The evidence of my own notebook is my proof. The evidence of your own records will be your proof. Parapsychologists know that precognitive dreams are a fact. This is not accepted generally in other scientific circles, however. Scientists will find proof themselves through a diligent study of their own dreams, and a program where dream events are systematically compared with actual physical events. They will not find such proof in their laboratories, however. There is only one laboratory in which dreams can be studied and evaluated, and that is the vastly complicated laboratory of the individual human personality.

The fact of precognitive dreams lends weight to the idea that the personality is not as tightly bound to space, time, or physical matter as is generally supposed. Your own dream records will bring this point home to you as nothing else can. This throws our conception of time into serious question. If the future existed separately, after the past and apart from the past, then it would be impossible to perceive future events either in dreams or in the waking state.

If time actually did exist in such a manner, then no emotional impetus could break that barrier between the future and the past. My own experiences convince me that portions of the future can be perceived, and that the popular conception of time is inadequate and misleading.

It may be that the ego can only perceive time as a series of moments, but part of the human personality can and does perceive events from a different perspective. It is not time itself, but the limitations of our ability to perceive time, that causes the difficulty. The reader may be interested in reading what the Seth Material says on this subject. Following is an excerpt from the material in which Seth first mentions what he calls "The Spacious Present." If time behaves as Seth maintains that it does, then there would be nothing supernatural in any kind of clairvoyance. Certainly clairvoyance cannot adequately be explained within the scope of current available theories. It is very possible that our whole idea of reality itself must be expanded.

In actuality there is only the spacious present, so spacious that it cannot be explored all at once in your terms. Hence, your arbitrary division of it into large rooms of past, present and future. You are in the spacious present now. You were in the spacious present in your yesterday, and you still will not have traveled through it in your tomorrow, or in eons of tomorrows.

In your terms the rate at which you discover the facets and realities of the spacious present become your physical or camouflage time. On your plane there must be physical manipulation. This also gives the illusion of past and future, and to you it appears that the present is a fleeting, almost ashen illusion in itself, beyond any true remembrance and beyond any but nostalgic recall. This is also caused by your physical camouflage system, in which physical materializations appear and grow, mature and disappear.

In the spacious present as it exists in actuality, all things that have existed still exist, and all things that shall exist in your tomorrow already do exist. You on your plane cannot experience such reality except in a very limited fashion, and you cannot experience such a reality spontaneously. But spontaneity is the quality of the spacious present.

As I have said that the walls of your house do not actually exist as such, so the divisions that you have placed within the spacious present do not exist. But as the walls of your house are experienced by your outer senses and serve to protect you against other physical camouflage materializations such as wind, rain and cold, so do the walls of past, present and future, erected by you as a different kind of camouflage pattern, protect you from inner forces and realities with which you are not as yet equipped to deal.

As a rule, when we have talked of camouflage in general we have been concerned with physical camouflage structures [physical objects]. There are, however, other camouflage patterns which do not exist as solid structures, but as ideas.

The idea of past, present and future is a necessary one on your plane, but this does not mean that time exists in the manner which you suppose. You are obsessed with the theory of beginning and end because in your situation camouflage constructions seem to have a beginning and an end.

For the same reason you are obsessed with the idea of cause and effect. With the illusion of successive time as you hold it the cause and effect theory follows: the one idea bringing forth the other. Here we have two of your most basic idea camouflage structures: your conception of time as a series of moments, and your idea of cause and effect.

There is no cause and effect in the terms in which you understand the words. Nor is there a succession of moments that follow one after the other. And without a succession of moments following one after another you can see that the idea of cause and effect becomes meaningless. An action in the present cannot be caused by an action in the past, and neither action can be the cause of future action, in a basic reality where neither past nor future exists.

The distortive illusion of successive moments and of the resulting conception of cause and effect, are both the result of observation by your outer physical senses, and are practical and useful on your plane. Therefore they have a certain validity, if for you only.

They represent a more or less true account of

the nature of your physical camouflage universe. But if they are understood as being limited to your own environment only, then your scientists would not attempt to use them as yardsticks to measure other realities.

There can be order without a succession of moments. There can be order, believe it or not, without your cause and effect. There can be order and there is order in spontaneity, and in the simultaneous existence of the spacious present.

You understand, of course, that the theory of successive moments works on your plane, or has worked so far. But as mankind grows more ambitious, then the idea will cease to work for him. It will actually be discarded on theoretical terms, while it is still utilized in its limited fashion in practical terms. You will, for example, continue to use watches long after your scientists discover that the theory of successive passage of moments is passé and antiquated.

CHAPTER 5

Various Kinds of Clairvoyant Dreams.

Further Experiments for You.

Are All Dreams Clairvoyant?

Our Experiments.

My own dream records convince me that in dreams we do receive information concerning future events—information we could not have received in any other manner. This data may come from the personal subconscious. It may come from deeper areas of the human personality. Regardless of its source, the information may be useful, and can sometimes be used in quite practical a manner. Your own dream records should allow you to perceive the ways in which you personally foresee future events. Most likely you have always had clairvoyant dreams, though you were not consciously aware of them. You were not in the habit of recalling any of your dreams except the most unusual ones. It is, therefore, not strange that you did not recognize the foreseen events when they occurred in physical reality.

There are many questions before us, however. Are all dreams clairvoyant to some extent? Do you perceive the future more clearly in your dreams at differing periods? Are there, for example, seasonal variations? Does your own subconscious distort what could be valid clairvoyant information?

You will be able to answer many of these questions for yourself. I can attempt to answer some of them for you in a general way. But the unique nature of the human personality means that your own dreams will have a distinctive overall make-up that is peculiarly your own. You can discover much about this dream framework of yours by studying your own dream notebook carefully.

First, as you keep your records, constantly compare your dreams against reality. As these records accumulate, you will begin to see patterns emerge. These will enable you to discover the characteristic ways in which you handle symbols within your dreams. You may discover, for example, that one month you recorded 30 dreams of which 3 seemed to be precognitive, while the following month you recorded only 10 dreams, and none appeared precognitive. Or you may discover that the opposite is true. You may find with time that in the autumn your rate of clairvoyant dreams is much higher than in the other seasons, or you may perceive no seasonal variations at all.

You will probably find, however, that your ability to recall your dreams in general has grown beyond expectation since you began training yourself to do so. The more dreams you remember, the more information you have with which to work. On those nights when you have one dream that seems to be precognitive, are some of the other dreams for that night also apt to be clairvoyant? Are you more receptive to precognitive information as it concerns your own family or friends? Or do you see events in which you have no personal involvement? No one can answer these questions for you, but it is important that you discover the answers. Only a careful evaluation of your own dream records can divulge them.

The results of my own evaluations may serve as a guide for you to follow. I began my own dream records in November 1963. The total of recalled dreams for 1964 was 104. Thirteen, or roughly 10 per cent of these contained precognitive elements. The incidents seen in these dreams later occurred in whole or part. There was no other way in which I could have received knowledge of these events. Thirteen—again roughly 10 per cent of the 104 dreams—involved psychic instruction of some sort. In them I was receiving lessons of various kinds. Five more dealt with psychic healing. These may have simply been caused by my conscious involvement with the field of ESP in general, or they may be attributable to definite communications between myself and others at a time when the ego could make no effective objection. The reader may decide for himself.

Note that in the whole year 1964 only 104 dreams were recorded. At the time, I was pleased to have remembered so many. Like most of you, previously I had recalled only the occasional spectacular dreams. In the next 5 months, however, from January 1965 to May 1965, a total of 174 dreams were recorded—proof that conditioning and practice are important. In 1964 an average of one dream per night was noted. Four dreams in one night was the highest number recorded. Obviously, many nights I remembered none. From January to May 1965 however, on those nights that I recalled dreams, the average was 3 dreams per night. On several instances 8 dreams for one night were recorded, and the highest number, reached in one night, was 13 dreams.

Of these 174 dreams reported from January to May 1965, 30 certainly seemed to contain valid clairvoyant information. Again, when I designate a dream as precognitive or clairvoyant, I mean that the dreams contained events which later checked out in whole or part: dreams that gave me information that I could not have received in any other way. Often I feel that a dream is precognitive, but there is no effective way to check whether or not the dream event actually happened in physical reality. In such a case, naturally the dream is not listed as precognitive.

My records make it plain that all such dreams are not of an unusual or startling variety. Many of them are quite commonplace and it may be for this reason that they are so often forgotten completely. Following are some examples from my own notebook. They will give you an idea as to how to grade your own dreams.

Here is an example of what I consider a good clairvoyant dream. On October 27, 1964, I dreamed that the old washing machine in the basement of our apartment house developed a leak. The dream was so insignificant that I almost discounted it. Although I told it to Robert at breakfast and wrote it down on a slip of paper which was inserted into my notebook, I forgot to write it down in the notebook itself until the following day. In the first place, no one had used the old washing machine in at least two years, as it was not in good working order.

On October 28, the morning after the dream, the water pipe connected to the machine broke. Water rushed through the washer, filled the tubs nearby, and gushed to the floor. The cellar was flooded to a depth of four inches. I discovered the flood myself. Checking, I learned that one of the tenants had decided to use the washer. When she left it, everything was in good order. I had not used the machine in several years and had no reason to suppose that anyone else would.

The following is another example of a dream that I personally consider a good clairvoyant one. On January 29 I recalled three dreams. One of these, too complicated to explain here, also seemed to be precognitive. The second dream was not clairvoyant. This is the third. The notebook account reads: "I wash sinks and care for a patient. A hospital-like dream."

Two nights after the dream a guest at our apartment suddenly developed a severe nose bleed. He bled profusely for over a half hour. On a past occasion, he informed us, he had needed a blood transfusion. We called the emergency room of the local hospital for instructions. As a result of his condition, we invited our guest to stay the night. It wasn't until I had washed the sinks several times that I remembered the dream, although it was written in my book. We washed bloody cloths, and cared for the patient.

The next dream made a strong impression upon me, but for several reasons I list it as a grade below the dreams just reported. One Saturday morning I awakened as Robert got out of bed. Then I fell asleep again to have the following dream, again quoted from my records: "I dreamed that Bill Macdonell dropped in to visit us early in the morning, before breakfast. He was on an errand in the neighborhood. Money was somehow connected with the errand. Seven cents? I am not sure. I think Bill owed the money to J. F."

When I awoke, I wrote the dream down, and told it to Robert. No sooner had I done so than there was a knock at the door. In came Bill Macdonell. He had been on an errand in the neighborhood—a doctor's appointment of which we had not known. We had not as yet eaten breakfast. Money was involved with the appointment, though not the seven cents of the dream. As we talked, Bill mentioned J. F.

Since Bill is a frequent visitor at our home, I did not give the dream as high a grading as the ones previously mentioned. Also the J. F. mentioned is a mutual acquaintance. There was nothing unusual in the fact that Bill mentioned him in our conversation. Bill said that he had thought of coming to see us while he was still in the doctor's office—this would be during the approximate time of my dream—so it is also possible that telepathy operated in this case.

In the dreams just related, however, the precognitive elements are fairly easy to recognize. They appear in a more or less pure form, undistorted. But what about the possibility that in some dreams valid clairvoyant information is mixed with other elements from the personal subconscious? My own records seem to show that this is often the case. A close study of your own notebook may also bring this to light.

The conclusions drawn in this chapter are based on a study of over 600 dreams, over 400 of mine and 200 of Robert's. The study so far extends over a two-year period. It is hoped that our information will be enlarged as this study is continued. The dreams themselves form the basic material.

Only a systematic investigation into the nature of dreams will lead to the discovery of their main ingredients and characteristics. My own dream records offer some evocative questions, and I am personally convinced that often legitimate clairvoyant information is interwound with other, subconscious, material. The work that I have

done so far leads me to believe that in dreams we sometimes not only receive data concerning future events, but
that we also work out in dreams probable solutions to
these events, facing them in the dream state before we deal
with them in physical reality.

In other words, it is possible that such dreams prepare
us ahead of time for events that will later occur. Because
of this interweaving of dream materials, without careful
records it is almost impossible to separate valid clairvoyant information from the whole dream action in many
cases. Enough similarities exist, however, so that examination can make such clairvoyant information clear. I am
concerned here not with dreams where precognitive events
are undisguised, but with dreams in which these events are
merged with dream solutions. We may, therefore, work
out our solutions to future events within dreams themselves, and choose in the dream situation the best solution
possible.

Some characteristics of clairvoyant dreams appear to
reveal themselves only after study. My own experience
leads me to believe that clairvoyant dreams have a tendency to occur in bunches. If one dream for a given night
has precognitive elements, then other dreams for that same
night also tend to be precognitive. Some examples from
my notebook will make these points clearer, and also
give you an idea of what to look for when you evaluate
your own dream records.

Consider the following dreams which all occurred
within a span of four nights.

Dream A 2/15/65 I see Robert fall down on the floor
with an attack of some sort; he falls in front of
the kitchen sink.

Dream B 2/15/65 I dream that we have a houseful
of company. An old friend, S. C., is one of the
guests.

Dream C 2/15/65 A table in a restaurant turns into
a bed. A group of older people watch as Robert and I straighten the bed, smooth down the
spread.

Dream D   2/16/65   I dream that Robert and I are
           hunting for an apartment.
Dream E   2/17/65   I dream about our landlord and
           the restaurant he owns, in connection with in-
           tegration.
Dream F   2/17/65   I dream that Robert and I must
           move out of our apartment.
Dream G   2/19/65   I dream that a woman editor comes
           to discuss the Seth Material.

Now, consider dreams C, D, E, F in the light of events
which happened immediately after this group of dreams.
My landlord also owns a restaurant. On February 18 he
visited our apartment to tell me that he was considering
selling the apartment house, and perhaps the restaurant
also. He had an appointment to show the house to prospective buyers, and was to meet with them. He requested
that I show them through our apartment. I consented,
and while he went to meet them, I cleared off the large
table where I write, straightened up the bed, and generally
tidied up our rooms. He returned with a group of older
people, who then inspected the apartment.

This group of dreams, C, D, E, F, all contained
elements that later showed themselves in an actual situation. They dealt with my landlord, the possibility of moving, older people and the straightening up of beds and
tables. I realize that the events are not precisely the same.
The dreams did give me notice however that our living
situation might be changed. If the landlord sold the apartment house, I was consciously worried that our rent
would be raised beyond our means. In one dream I saw
Robert and myself looking for a new apartment. While
we did not do so, and the deal did not go through, I am
convinced that in that dream I was working out possible
solutions to the problem that was foreseen.

Now consider dreams A and B, both of the same night.
In one, I see Robert fall down to the floor, in an attack
of some kind. In another, the house is full of company,
including S. C. The dreams occurred on February 15. On
March 24, over a month later, Robert woke up, walked

into the bathroom, and fell to the floor in a sudden faint in front of the shower. On that same day we had more company than we usually have in two weeks' time. As I tried to care for Robert, who had a particularly bad virus, company kept arriving. Among the visitors was S. C. We had seen her only twice in eight years. If the dream had not been in my records—and had the similarity between the dream and the actual events not been emphasized by the events all happening on the same day (as the dreams took place in the same night)—I never would have been aware of the connection.

Here I would like to add a note about the blocking of disturbing dreams. The dream concerning Robert's illness frightened me to such an extent that I caught myself thinking: "I won't remember this one. I don't like the sound of it." Then, catching myself, I forced myself to write it down at once. Otherwise it would have been forgotten—on purpose.

Yet that dream, like the moving dream, helped me to prepare for physical events that later occurred. The moving dreams gave generalized information concerning the possibility that our living conditions might be changed. I would have been much more nervous on being informed of our landlord's plans, if a dream had not already advised me of them, and if I had not already faced the possibility of moving by dreaming that we looked for another apartment. Robert's attack, known about in advance, also prepared me psychologically for his illness.

This leaves one other dream, of February 19, in which a woman editor arrived to discuss the Seth Material. At the time of the dream I was not dealing with any women editors. The Seth Material had been at Frederick Fell Inc. for over five months. Robert wrote requesting the return of the material. On March 7 we received a letter from a woman editor who had taken a position with the publishing house in the meantime. She had sent me a card which I had never received. In the letter she discussed the Seth Material as well as this manuscript. She did not actually visit me in person, however.

During the entire time records have been kept, no other

dreams concerning woman editors, S. C., moving, or illnesses were noted. They are included in this book because they contained recognizable elements of events that later happened, but they lacked the clear-cut precision of dreams mentioned earlier. At the same time they seem to suggest that in dreams we not only foresee some future events, but try to solve future problems in the dream situation.

The similarities between the dream events and the physical events just mentioned could easily be laid to chance. These are not the only examples of such bunched dreams, however. My notebook presents many others, all of which seem to give different facets of an actual later situation. The foreseen event may be mixed in with other dreams in which we work out solutions. For this reason, many clairvoyant dreams would not at first appear to be such, while study might allow us to separate the various dream elements and make the connections clear.

There is no other adequate manner to discover the nature and characteristics of dreams except by examining the stuff of dreams themselves. An examination of your own dream records will show your personal method of blending various dream elements. Experience will then allow you to separate clairvoyant data when it is not crystal clear. To bend over backwards in an effort to accept all dreams as precognitive will only confuse the issue. Integrity and common sense are necessary to your own evaluations.

Close investigation of mixed dreams may add more to our knowledge of human personality and potentials than a study of more clear-cut clairvoyant dreams, since such a study would be deeply involved with the working of the inner self, not only in perceiving precognitive data but in using it in practical terms. If we foresee events in dreams—and also interpret them, and try to work out various solutions to them—then the dreaming state is more practical than we have ever supposed.

Now what about deliberate distortion of valid precognitive information in dreams? Is it possible that often we receive knowledge of future events and then distort it in dreams? I think this is very possible, and when this occurs it adds to the difficulty of assessing exactly how much data we do receive. In these cases, the precognitive information may be completely used up or translated by the personal subconscious into another sort of dream drama. There are many reasons for the subconscious to distort such material. The nature of the event may be unpleasant. If this is so, the information may come through clearly simply because it requires some future definite action on our part which cannot be avoided. Or, a foreseen unpleasant event may be one requiring no action on our part, and we therefore feel we can safely distort it. The event may present problems of long standing, or the information simply may not come in sufficiently strong enough to force its recognition.

Here are some examples that will show you what I mean. Again we have a bunched sequence: all three dreams occurred on the same evening, February 18, 1964.

Dream A   I enter the office of two magazine publishers. I am uneasy as I open the door. There is a distinct feeling that I have made no sale. There is some trouble on the landing outside.

Dream B   I get a phone call from a strange woman, or I call her. She doesn't want to be bothered. Surprised, I tell her that my mother gave me her number and asked me to call.

Dream C   A dream about an old friend, Mrs. G.

The day after these dreams a magazine rejected a story of mine, "The Outsider." Remember that my notation of the dream included the word "outside." The dream did let me know, at the very least, that a story had been rejected.

The same day I received a letter from my mother in which she devoted most of her remarks to a discussion of a woman with whom I am not acquainted, a stranger. She apologized in the letter for devoting so much of it to this woman. My mother also gave me some news of the old friend, Mrs. G.

Once more, such similarities can easily be dismissed

as chance, particularly since precognitive elements are not clearly given. My notebook shows so many cases like these, however, that it seems we must consider the possibility that many dreams, not obviously precognitive, may nevertheless contain valid clairvoyant information which is distorted by the personality for its own reasons.

I had not seen my old friend Mrs. G. in many years, and we did not part under pleasant circumstances. Of course, the rejection of a story is never happy news. Perhaps unconsciously I was jealous because my mother devoted so much space in her letter to a woman I do not know. All in all, however, no immediate action was necessary on my part as far as the actual events were concerned. It is possible that I simply distorted the material. Nevertheless, I was not surprised to receive my mother's letter with mention of Mrs. G., nor was I surprised to find the rejection in the day's mail.

Precognitive elements may show themselves, then, in at least three kinds of dreams: those in which the clairvoyant information is clear, concise and unmistakable; those in which it is mixed with dream dramas in which solutions to the problems involved are worked out; and those in which the information is distorted by the subconscious to some considerable degree.

A study of your own dream records will allow you to recognize these tendencies. Obviously it is also necessary to keep check of daily events, and compare them with the dream events. It will not help to seize upon every small coincidence and label it precognitive. On the other hand, it will serve no purpose to ignore the possibilities that the second two types of dreams seem to present.

Are all dreams clairvoyant then? If you dream of a death in the family, will actual death necessarily result? It seems clear that all dreams are not clairvoyant. A dream concerning a death, for example, may be merely the expression of subconscious concern with the inevitability of death. Such a dream may represent a repressed wish that the person involved would in fact be struck dead—a wish that is released harmlessly enough by the sleeping self. Do not be alarmed by these dreams when they occur. They may only reflect a momentary drop of spirits on your part.

Before we leave the subject of dreams, let us very briefly consider the possibility that some of them contain telepathic communications. My own records barely hint at this connection between dreams and telepathy. One situation in particular, however, aroused my interest in this respect. In a dream I read a critical article concerning the Seth Material. At precisely this time, Robert woke me up. He said angrily, "Did you read that article about the Seth Material?"

"What article?" I said, instantly interested. But he had either been talking in his sleep or had awakened only for an instant. The incident, of course, proves nothing. Since then, however, I have heard of other similar experiences and I find the whole matter intriguing. It is easily possible that Robert talked in his sleep, mentioned an article of which he was dreaming, and prompted me to have the same sort of dream.

There is also the possibility that in dreams we receive suggestions which we then react to in waking life. The waking experience would then appear to be clairvoyant when it was not. Only careful investigations of such dream material can give us any definite answers to all the questions here presented.

For your own experiments, then, continue your dream notebook, making sure that you date all dreams and events. Constantly check daily happenings against your dreams. Evaluate the contents of your notebook every month. In this evaluation look for the following:

A. Number of dreams recorded. This will enable you to chart your own progress.

B. Number of dreams that seem to be precognitive. This should include dreams that appear to be clearly clairvoyant; dreams in which the clairvoyant elements are mixed with attempts at solution of problems connected with foreseen events; and dreams which contain clairvoyant elements that are distorted by the subconscious.

C. The general nature of the precognitive material you

usually receive. Is it apt to be of a personal nature, for example? Or do you foresee events in which you may not take part—political events, newspaper headlines, etc.

D. A bunching up of precognitive dreams. Look also for seasonal variations.

E. Any unifying dream symbols which may appear in various ways in your dreams, or within any given dream series. These will be briefly explained in the excerpts from the Seth Material which follow. The excerpts are concerned with dreams and clairvoyance, and are interesting from several viewpoints.

Excerpts from Session 45

If cause and effect were an absolute law, then continuity would also have to be an absolute law, and all or any evidence of clairvoyance would be absolutely impossible. It is only because there is basically no cause and effect, but merely apparent cause and effect, and no past, present and future, that clairvoyance is possible in your universe.

While awareness of clairvoyance is fairly rare, it does exist, and though watered down in most instances, it is a natural method of warning individuals of happenings with which their own physical senses would not be familiar. It is a natural method of protecting the individual through an inner knowledge of events. Without constant clairvoyance on the part of every man and woman, existence on your plane would involve such inner psychological insecurity that it would be completely unbearable.

Individuals are always warned of disasters, so that the organism can prepare itself ahead of

time. The time of death is known. Consciously
this kind of knowledge is not given to the ego for
obvious reasons, but every organism through its
inner senses is equipped with subconscious knowledge of personal disasters, deaths, and so forth,
the personality deciding itself beforehand what it
considers disastrous. The members of the species
knows in advance of their wars. As telepathy
operates constantly at a subconscious level as a
basis for all language and communication, so
clairvoyance operates continually so that the physical organism can prepare itself to meet its challenges.

This is quite enough for one session, my
pigeons . . .

Excerpts from Session 93

Considerable confusion can result if a dream
from one level of the subconscious is interpreted
in the light of data which belongs to another level
entirely. Many individuals feel easier with certain
subconscious aspects, with the result that they may
be more aware of dreams that originate in particular subconscious areas, and relatively unaware
of dreams originating in other areas.

We will find in many cases, most of all, dreams
originating in the layer of personal subconscious,
the most simple being those that have immediate
reference to daily conscious life. While such a
dream is less complex than others, it is nevertheless an amazing construction . . . While it may

seem that all dreams are random conglomerations of unrelated symbols or events, we will see that one of the most important attributes of any dream is, indeed, discrimination.

For out of a seemingly endless number of possibilities, our individual dreamer actually discriminates with great care, choosing only those dream objects that best serve his purposes. Even a simple dream concerned with trivial daily events is in reality much more.

The dream objects are, in fact, chosen with such precise discrimination that on deep examination they will be seen to embody not only data concerning the daily conscious existence, but one and every dream object may be seen to apply to many levels of the subconscious at once.

These dream objects are so cunningly, almost slyly chosen, that the simplest of them may refer to instances in the existence; to personally [subconsciously] feared objects or instances; to desired or feared objects or instances from past lives. Such dream objects may also be methods with which the inner self warns the personality of possible future disasters or disappointments.

One dream object, then, may simultaneously represent a simple daily and familiar portion of conscious life, a strongly feared or desired portion of the immediately subconscious layer, an event or object from a past life, or a feared or desired future event, as the case may be.

An equation exists here. One dream object has

reality in four or five different layers of reality simultaneously: the object being more than itself, and equal to realities that have existed or will exist; the past and future being therefore contained simultaneously within the dream object by virtue of a quite real psychic contraction and expansion.

The expansion is the dream. The contraction is the return of the dream elements back into the original single object, that is, the dream object from which the equation originated. As, for example, all numbers originate from the number one.

Each dream, first of all, begins with psychic energy which the dreamer transforms not into physical matter but into a reality every bit as functional and as real. He forms the idea into a dream object or event with amazing discrimination, so that the object or event itself gains existence, and exists in various dimensions.

It does not *seem* to exist in various dimensions. It does in actuality so exist. If a dream object or event straddles what you call not only time but space, and if, as I say, dream objects and creations maintain some independence from the dream, then you can see that although the dreamer creates his dreams for his own purposes, he nevertheless projects them outward in a psychic expansion.

The expansion, again, occurs as the dream drama is acted out. For the dreamer, a contraction occurs as he is finished with the events or drama for his own purposes, but no energy can be taken back.

Energy projected into any kind of a construction cannot be recalled, but must follow the laws of the particular form into which it has been for the moment molded. Therefore, when the dreamer contracts his multirealistic objects backward, ending for himself the dream that he has constructed, he ends it for himself only. The reality of the dream continues. I do not care if this idea now appears impossible, either to you and Ruburt or to others. The fact remains that it is so.

The fact also remains that on other levels but conscious ones, you and every individual knows that the dream world is indeed constructed by the inner self with utmost care, with precision known only to the intuitions. And each individual knows that such a splendid creation as this then exists beyond the self that was its origin.

CHAPTER 6

Telepathy.
Do We Pick Up the Thoughts of Others?
Experiments for You to Try.

Contact a distant relative or friend without writing a letter or using a telephone? This may sound improbable, yet it is very possible that all of us do this on a subconscious level a good deal of the time. In fact, such telepathic messages may be received so easily and smoothly that we act on them automatically, without giving them any conscious attention at all.

The Russians have been experimenting with telepathy as a method of communication between Earth and space vehicles. The U.S. government is experimenting in the transmission of telepathic commands to volunteers aboard Polaris submarines. Telepathy could conceivably end up as a weapon in some future cold war.

But what about telepathy (thought transference) in ordinary everyday life? Here are some experiences told to me by a neighbor, a teacher in his thirties. Coincidence is a possible explanation for any one instance, yet when we consider groups of such happenings, certain patterns seem to present themselves which make coincidence less likely as an explanation.

One weekend morning this neighbor felt a sudden strong impulse to visit his sister. He felt particularly impelled to go to her house for dinner that evening, though she lived forty miles away, and he was not in the habit of making such a trip unless he planned to stay for a longer period of time.

That afternoon he finally decided to make the drive. As he left his apartment, the phone rang and he returned to answer it. His sister was calling him. She asked him to drive down for dinner, saying that she had thought about calling him all morning, but hesitated. She did not think that he would want to make such a long trip for such a short visit. Finally she had decided to call. Apparently in this case, the actual phone call was quite unnecessary. My neighbor had already received the message, and was acting upon it.

On another occasion this same gentleman made up his mind to visit his brother, who also lived in a town about forty miles away. Although he had looked forward to making the trip, he suddenly felt an urge to put it off for a while and take a short drive around town. When he returned home, the phone was ringing. The call was from his brother who was at the local airport. He had flown to Elmira purposely to see my neighbor. The two see each other infrequently. Had the teacher made the automobile journey, he would have missed his brother entirely. Only his illogical urge to put the trip off for a while made the meeting possible.

Here are some experiences of my own. These particular incidents and the ones just mentioned represent fairly insignificant occurrences. We often shrug them off as coincidence, without giving them further thought or consideration. Later in this chapter we will be concerned with some experiences that are not so easy to forget.

Last New Year's Eve, Robert and I met a young couple, call them the X's, at a party. The following afternoon as I sat in the living room, someone knocked at the door. Instantly I knew that Mr. X was at the door, and that his wife was not with him. This proved to be the case.

One afternoon later in the year, Robert was late coming home for lunch. The idea suddenly came to me that he had quit his job, though there was no reason for him to do so particularly, and he had not spoken of doing so. I was concerned, thinking that if he left his position as commercial artist, we might have to leave town as he works only on a part-time basis, and in a small town such situations are difficult to find. Yet the idea was distinct: he had quit his job and we were moving out of town.

No sooner had I received these thoughts than Robert returned. Our friend, Mr. X, was with him. Mr. X had come to see us purposely to tell us that just moments before he had quit his job. He and his wife were moving out of town. He had met Robert outside the apartment house, on his way to see us. Here, apparently, I had picked up Mr. X's thought, but because I was consciously concerned with Robert's tardiness, I attributed the message to him.

Here is another instance. A friend gave me a coat which she had discarded. The friend then moved away. A year passed. I had never worn the coat. One day last winter, I decided to wear it downtown. As I put the coat on, I thought: "If I wear this, I'll probably meet A. R. who will remember the coat and know it is a hand-me-down. (A. R. had been present when the coat was given to me.) I was tempted to take the coat off, but as I never met A. R. on any of my trips downtown, I decided it was idiotic to suppose that I would meet him on this occasion. So I wore the coat. When I completed my errands, I stopped in to see another friend, who works in a store. I had no sooner put my hand on the glass door to enter, when I saw A. R. talking to my friend. I had visited the friend often in the store and A. R. had never been present.

The following is another simple incident. Again, this experience could also involve mere coincidence. At 7:45 one morning as I did the dishes, I suddenly decided to return a neighbor's plate that I had borrowed. The thought was strong that I should do so. I picked it up and started for the door. Then, remembering the early hour, I put the plate down. Just as I did so, there was a knock at the door. This same neighbor called, wanting to borrow something from me. In our five years as neighbors, he has never knocked at the door so early in the morning. I gave him the plate.

One evening I went to a nearby grocery store, telling

Robert I would return immediately. On my way back
I remembered that a friend had a book of mine which
he had borrowed but not returned. I decided to stop and
see if he was finished with it. He is a professional man,
with his office in his home. The book was in his office. As
he was busy, I had coffee with his wife. We talked for an
hour. It was winter, and a dark night. Nervously I thought
that Robert would be concerned about me by now, since
I usually return from the store at once. My eyes darted
to the clock. It was 7 P.M. Finally I decided not to wait
any longer. When I reached home, without speaking
Robert gave me a piece of paper. On it was written: "7
P.M. Strong feeling that Jane is at Dr. X's."

Now Robert did know the man had a book of mine,
but I had passed his house often in the past without ever
stopping to get it. Other friends of ours lived between
our apartment and the store. I could have stopped to see
any one of them.

Most readers can recall many such experiences of
their own. At the time the incidents impress us to some
degree, but we feel we can prove nothing by such accounts.
They could be adequately explained by many other means
besides telepathy. Telepathy is, however, one possible
explanation and it should not be entirely discounted
simply because it is not the only one.

The following incident is, however, somewhat more
difficult to assign as the result of chance or coincidence.
One night as I lay in bed, half asleep and half awake, I
heard these words inside my head: "Yeah, but it's darned
expensive. Who the devil's going to pay for it? Aren't
there foundations or something to cover this sort of
thing?" The voice was instantly familiar to me as belonging to a friend who was out of town at the time. He
sounded angry and shocked. I told Robert what I had
heard, immediately wrote the exact words down and
noted the time and date. It was a few minutes past 1 A.M.

The next day I tried to figure out what must have happened. The man's father was ill. Perhaps Mr. M was
worried about a possible opeation that his father might
have to undergo. Three days later my friend returned. As

Robert and I visited him, I asked about the father and was told that his condition was the same. "He doesn't need an operation or anything, does he?" I asked. Puzzled, Mr. M answered in the negative. I was ready to forget the whole thing. Instead, luckily, I told Mr. and Mrs. M what I had heard.

It was my turn to be surprised. The night of my experience the M's had been in a resort area. They left a cocktail lounge at 1 A.M., the closing hour, to walk the short distance to their nearby motel. The motel manager walked with them. Outside, they found the grounds littered with junk. Vandals had thrown the expensive lawn furniture into the swimming pool, along with garbage. The area was a shambles. It was in answer to the manager's denunciation of the damage that Mr. M said, "Yeah, but it's damned expensive [damage]. Who the devil's going to pay for it? Aren't there foundations or something to cover this sort of thing?" By foundations he meant insurance.

Coincidence seems a pretty weak explanation for this sort of incident. In some manner I apparently tuned into a situation many miles away, and picked up Mr. M's angry comment. Had this information been received in a dream, incidentally, it is very possible that I would have incorporated my own hospital explanation into the dream itself, distorting it beyond recognition. For this reason, whenever you write down such experiences, be certain that you record only the exact words that you hear.

The following is another example which can hardly be attributed to chance or coincidence alone. It happened under the same circumstances as those in Mr. M's case. It took place late at night. Again I was half awake and half asleep. Suddenly I realized that my mind contained the image of a newspaper article. I had been reading it, and comparing the information on it with another piece of paper. The article said that a friend, Mr. X, had been offered or given a promotion at his place of business, that a reorganization would take place, and that another friend who also worked there, a Mr. K, would also be involved. When I realized what was happening, the newspaper article and the other piece of paper both vanished. I wrote the information down at once, and told Robert what I had seen.

The following day Mrs. X came to call. As best I could, I related my experience, and showed her the notations I had made. Surprised, she told me that her husband was being considered for a promotion in his office, but the whole affair was highly secret. Only those directly concerned knew anything about it. Even most of the office staff was ignorant of the situation, but a reorganization was definitely taking place. She did not know that any change was planned for Mr. K.

Two and a half weeks later, Mr. K was suddenly transferred to another location, due to the fact that another man had resigned his position. No newspaper article actually appeared, however. Mr. X did not accept the promotion offered. Both men worked at a newspaper office. This, I imagine, explains why I saw a newspaper article. By this means the place of business was made clear to me.

This last instance involved sight rather than sound: I saw, rather than heard, the information. The following experience involved something with which I am sure many of my readers have been familiar in their own lives: a voice. How many times have you been certain that someone called your name, when you were alone? In most cases, we merely think that we are hearing things, shake our heads, and forget the incident. Actually I was working on this very chapter when suddenly I was certain that a woman called my name. The voice seemed to come from inside my head, rather than from my physical environment. I looked out the window, however, to see if anyone was in the yard. It was empty. I was alone in the apartment. Most of the other tenants were at work. In any case, our apartment house is old and sturdy. Sounds do not carry.

Because I have trained myself to make a note of such incidents, no matter how insignificant they seem, I wrote the experience down in my notebook, and the time, 9:15 A.M. Then, forgetting it, I returned to my writing.

Twenty minutes or so later, the impulse suddenly struck me to call my friend Mrs. S. Naturally, I thought that this was my own idea, though it came out of the blue, so to speak. We do not have a phone. I used a neighbor's to make the call. Mrs. S answered, telling me that she and her husband had just been speaking of me. She had some news she wanted to tell me, and she had been wishing that I had a phone so she could reach me.

It wasn't until I returned to my typewriter that I remembered the woman's voice I had heard. Mrs. S had told me that the conversation with her husband had begun when he came down for coffee, a little after 9 A.M. The earlier notation concerning the voice had completely slipped my mind.

On another occasion as I sat working, I felt a sudden urge to call Peggy Gallagher, another friend, at the newspaper, or to visit her there. Rarely do I leave the house once I have settled down to work. However, the impulse to see Peggy was a strong one. Looking at the clock, I saw that it was 9:30. Since I had begun working at 8 A.M., I decided that at 10 I would walk down to visit her. When she saw me, she told me she had been concentrating on me since 9:30 when I first felt the urge to see her. We had some business together and she had been anxious to contact me. Since I have no phone and she knew that I was working on this book, she decided to try telepathy. Again, I thought that going down to see her had been my own idea.

Instances of what certainly seem to involve telepathy have happened during the Seth sessions. One night, for example, Seth answered a witness's questions before the man asked them. We had missed our regularly scheduled session the evening before. Mr. Y, who was only an acquaintance at the time, dropped in to call. As we sat chatting with our guest, I felt that Seth wanted to make up the missed session.

We had never had a witness before. Nervously I wondered what would happen. Seth was not at all concerned. The session began, guest or no guest. We had a few minutes' notice, so we gave our guest a brief idea of what the sessions were. Robert gave Mr. Y some paper and a pen, for him to write down any questions that came to mind. He never got the chance to use the pen. Unknown to me, Seth answered all his questions in the order in which he thought of them. No suggestion was given to our guest that Seth could or would do so. The idea had never entered our heads. The sessions were still very new to us at that time.

Our guest was intrigued. He returned for a later session, asking Seth about problems in his professional life. Seth answered in his usual lively fashion. Toward the end of the monologue, he mentioned that Mr. Y had abilities along electronic lines that were not being used, and suggested that he become a ham radio operator. When the session was over, Mr. Y told us that the basement of his house was filled with various kinds of electronic equipment. He had often thought of becoming a ham operator, but had not done so because of the expense. Mr. Y lives in a distant city which we have never visited. We could not have seen his home. He had never mentioned his interest in electronics to us, nor did he seem like a man who would have such interests.

The term "telepathy" has been used mainly to express what can best be called "thought transference," without communication through usual methods. Clairvoyance has generally been used to express extrasensory knowledge of future events. But in my experience, the two are so closely related that many times it is difficult to distinguish between them. Nor do the particular terms themselves matter. They only serve to make an artificial distinction in what is basically one ESP function. Since the two designations are in general use, however, we will use them here.

There are certain characteristics that seem to be involved with instances of both clairvoyance and telepathy. Before we discuss some experiments for you to try on your own, let us consider some of these characteristics. Extrasensory perceptions in general seem to occur when the conscious mind is diverted. Conscious concentration is apt to inhibit such phenomena. Telepathy seems to n emotional basis in many instances. We appear to up the thoughts of those with whom we are psychologically close. Probably we cannot will ourselves to transmit or receive a telepathic communication. We can, I believe, allow ourselves to do so.

It is important that you become familiar with those parts of the mind through which such communications must come. Here is a simple experiment that will let you do so. For ten minutes each day, sit or lie quietly. Listen to your own conscious thoughts. Do not tamper with them or judge them. Just listen, objectively. This is your stream of consciousness, the flow of thoughts that rush through your mind almost constantly. Sometimes we are aware of them, but usually only when we are quiet.

When you have learned to distinguish this stream of consciousness, ignore it. You will then discover disconnected thoughts and images just beneath it. Without too much difficulty, you will find that the stream of consciousness will no longer concern you. You will become aware of what lies beneath. You may hear words that seem meaningless. You may see quick pictures glow and fade.

Pretend that your mind is like an ocean. You are traveling in a diving outfit, slowly, down into it. First you pass the stream of consciousness which flows just beneath the surface. Then you reach the next level where the thoughts and images are less familiar, like exotic fish dashing past. Do not attempt to grab hold of these words or images, or they will elude you. Simply observe them.

You will need all your powers of perception. You may hear voices. They may be clear enough to hear for a moment, then fade away. Be patient. Do not strain to see or hear. Quietly observe and listen.

When you grow used to this experience, then you will become acclimated to the new conditions. You may discover that certain images will last longer than others. You may see them more clearly. Words that seemed jumbled before may now be distinct. They may involve, as my friends' words did for me, situations existing in present time but miles away in space. They may involve the future or the past. Until you listen and watch you will never know.

Some images will simply be meaningless. Sometimes you will see or hear nothing. Some pictures may involve people whom you do not know. They may be the result of imagination, or they may be concerned with valid perceptions of actual people which are relatively impossible to check upon. If you hear voices you recognize, or words that make sense, write them down. If you see images of acquaintances or friends, write a description of what you see. Later make an attempt to question the people concerned as to the meaning of your experience.

Many times I could not know I was receiving legitimate information until I checked with the persons involved. You cannot take it for granted that images or words have validity unless you are able to verify them in one way or another. The experiment itself will allow you to reach the same sort of suspension between walking and sleeping that you ordinarily experience in bed at night. This is a state in which telepathic communications may be most often received, and in which some of mine have occurred.

All the words and images will not be telepathic by any means. Some may be simple subconscious fabrications; the inner mind at spontaneous play. Practice will undoubtedly help you develop some ability to distinguish between perceptions coming from various sources. My own experience allows me to discriminate somewhat in selecting which images are significant and which are not. Objective and systematic checking of such information remains the only definite way to establish validity.

Actually, your intuitive feeling about any given experience may be more reliable than your conscious evaluation. Several times I discounted words that popped into my head when I was in this suspended state, discarding them because they seemed unlikely to have meaning. Later, when events happened to back them up, I was at a loss because I had neglected to write them down. At other times I was consciously certain that the same sort of information was valid and, when I checked with the persons involved, it was not.

Our next experiments involve another notebook. This notebook should soon become as intriguing and important to you as your dream notebook. Not only that, but you may discover, as I did, that similarities exist between your dreams and the incidents you will record.

Earlier in this chapter we discussed those seemingly insignificant occurrences that frequently startle us with their resemblance to inner thoughts we have had immediately before the events happened. Almost everyone has experienced such cases in his own life. How many times have you thought of a particular friend only to have him or her ring you up on the telephone, at the same time or only seconds after the thought? How many times have you thought that someone called your name even though you were alone, and no one was nearby to call out to you?

From now on, write down all such instances. Date each entry. Also record any strong hunches or thoughts that pop into your head if they seem unrelated to what you are doing at the time. Check constantly to see if there is any relationship between your hunches and daily events. If you hear someone call your name, write the fact down, then keep careful watch on events for the rest of the day; someone may want to get in touch with you. You may get a letter or phone call that will make the reason for the voice clear.

If the phone rings and you know who is calling before you pick up the receiver, make note of this. Include the name of the person who called, and the date. How many times a week does this happen? Do you always know when certain people will call you on the telephone? Or, now that you are actually writing down such instances, do you discover that you were not right half as often as you thought you were? These questions you will be able to answer for yourself.

Is there a correlation between your precognitive dreams and telepathic flashes? Are they both apt to be more numerous at certain times? Keep all these questions in mind. Check the two notebooks against each other. Answers to such queries can tell us much about the nature of the human personality and of the mind. Also a lot of human work will remain undone.

It is very difficult to prove that any one instance is a valid telepathic communication, and each such event must be studied alone. But if significant experiences of this nature accumulate in your notebook, if they are faithfully and honestly recorded and carefully checked out, then the very bulk of the material itself may suggest that telepathy and not coincidence is involved.

Many of my clairvoyant dreams are implemented by telepathic flashes. Often the information received in dreams is reinforced by words I hear in my head. It seems to make no difference whether the dream or telepathic flash happens first in time. When two such instances occur, both pertaining to the same physical event, then to me this adds to the validity of both the dream and the telepathic flash.

You may very well find the same sort of connection between some of your precognitive dreams and the words or thoughts that come to you while you are doing something else. Only by keeping careful records, however, can you discover such similarities. It is precisely because ESP is apt to be spontaneous that we must be so disciplined in our recording of it. More will be said later in this book concerning the reinforcement that seems to occur between various extrasensory perceptions.

Our next experiment involves the use of official ESP cards, for the testing of extrasensory perception. These can be purchased through the mail from the Parapsychology Department, Duke University, Durham, N.C. Instructions are included for the very small price of one dollar. Twenty-five record sheets come with the cards and the cards can be used for several different tests.

It is possible to make up your own set of cards, but there are good reasons for purchasing the official ones. For one thing, the cards are absolutely uniform in size and thickness. The backs are opaque, and identical, lessening the possibility that subconscious cues might be received that would affect the scores. The pack is composed of 25 cards made up of five symbols: star, waves, cross or plus sign, circle, and square.

When you get the cards, you should construct a small screen of heavy cardboard or any such suitable material to shield the person who gives the tests (the operator) from the person who takes the tests (the subject). The operator handles the cards and the subject tries to ascertain the way they fall in the deck. All scores are written down on the record sheets.

A chance score, running through the cards once (one run), would be five. Chance alone, then, would allow the subject to guess five out of the 25 cards correctly. Anything above this score could be considered as being above chance. However, a minimum of ten runs is necessary, and preferably many more. On the first three runs, for example, you may get a high score, while your score for the next seven runs could go below chance, cutting your total score considerably.

I suggest that you run through the cards frequently. Note in your records the mood you were in when you took each test, the time of the day the test was tried, even the condition of the weather. We simply do not know how ESP works, and what various conditions influence it. Your own results can answer many questions for you. Do you do better with the cards when you are in a good mood? A bad mood? Does the weather seem to have an effect on your scores? If science could discover the conditions in which extrasensory perceptions operate best, then experiments could be set up that would be most useful in the attempt to put ESP on some kind of predictable basis.

Try the cards out on relatives and friends. Keep track of all scores. Do not run through the cards so many times at one sitting that you become tired. Always follow the instructions to the letter. If you got significant scores without the screen, for example, your scores should be discounted because the conditions for the tests were not properly complied with.

In our own experiments with the cards, I once made the good score of calling 67 cards correctly on a clairvoyance test. For this particular test, the subject tries to guess the order of the cards in the pack as the pack lies face down upon the table. The cards themselves are not touched. A score of 50 would have been chance. However, other scores in different runs lowered my total score considerably. Robert once gave correct calls for 12 of 25 cards. We have not emphasized the cards in our own investigations.

Some workers in the field of ESP have had excellent results using the cards. Others have not. It is important that you keep your own initiative high, and not become bored with the repetition. Try the tests in a spirit of fun. Extrasensory perceptions have a spontaneous nature. Often they come when we least expect them. Have a scientific attitude when you judge the results of all the experiments in this book. First, however, you must allow yourself the inner freedom that is necessary to "pick up" perceptions that do not come through the physical senses.

There are numerous experiments that you can initiate for yourself. For example, try having one person make a drawing of a simple object or symbol on a piece of paper while he is in another room. Then try to draw the exact object or symbol. Many may join in this simple experiment. Always keep records. Number the original drawing I or O for original, or use any other designation which will keep your records clear.

And remember your notebook. Refuse to accept coincidence as the only explanation for everything you do not understand. Write such incidents in your records. Does it seem that your letters often cross other letters in the mail, for example? If you write a friend on Wednesday, do you often get a letter from him on Thursday, before he may even have received yours? Or is this only your imagination? Keep notes and find out for yourself. Don't take anything for granted.

Try to contact a distant friend or relative without using the telephone or taking advantage of the more usual methods of communication. If you follow these experiments, if you take the time and effort to examine your own inner self, you may find yourself able to do just that.

Following are some excerpts from the Seth Material in which Seth discusses telepathy in general and the ways in which thoughts are transmitted from the sender (A) to the receiver (B).

Excerpts from Session 136

I have said that there are no duplicates. Yet, you may say, are not some thoughts duplicates? The variations may indeed be slight, but variations are always present. A thought transmitted knowingly or unknowingly by A is not precisely the same thought when it reaches receiver B.

The thought originally held by A is still retained by A, yet a seemingly identical thought reaches B. A has lost nothing. That is, in trying to send the thought, in trying to duplicate the thought, A still retains it. So what is passed on to receiver B? This is rather important, since an explanation will do much to account for the frequent difference that occurs in telepathic communications.

Whether or not A, the sender, knowingly transmits this apparent duplicate, at the point of its transmission, the sender forms an electrical impulse pattern that is supposed to duplicate the original thought. But no such identical duplication is possible, as far as I know, within reality of any kind.

A side note: identical twins are hardly identical, for example.

As soon as the attempt is made to duplicate the

thought, we find the attempt itself strains and pulls; the impulse changes minutely, or to a greater degree. The point I want to make is that any attempt at duplication actually forces the impulses to line up in a different pattern. When B receives the thought it is already a new thought, bearing great resemblance to the original. But it is not the original thought.

Prime identities cannot be duplicated. Exact duplication is always an effect of insufficient knowledge. In some cases two thoughts may appear identical, but whether or not examination can show it, such exact duplication is impossible. Now when receiver B receives a transmitted thought, he may react and interpret that part of the thought that is similar to the original.

He may, on the other hand, react to and interpret that portion of the thought that is not similar. He may react to and interpret the similarity or the difference. His reactions depend upon several circumstances, including the intensity of the electrical pulsations that compose the thought, and his own inner facility in reacting to particular ranges of intensities.

Habitually, individuals establish overall frequencies that they are able to handle, for various reasons that I have explained earlier. An individual will therefore feel more at home operating within certain frequencies. The original thought is used as a pattern for the creation of a new electrical reality which may or may not be directed at any given receiver. It is obvious that the attempt to duplicate is present: were it not for this attempt to duplicate, then there would be little similarity between any separate identities.

The nature of the thought that is received by B is determined by many factors. We shall consider but a few of these. These include the original intensity of the thought as A possesses it; A's ability to duplicate the thought as far as possible; the relative stability of the electrical thought unit as it is formed by A; the familiarity or unfamiliarity of the range of frequencies that compose the thought to any intended receiver.

The receiver will understand and interpret in general the intensity range he is in the habit of using himself. Some, or a portion of the transmitted thought, may fall within his range and some may not. He may pick up the portions of the thought which are similar to the original thought, in which case some scientific proof of sorts can be achieved. It can happen, however, that the dissimilarity is what falls within his particular accustomed range, in which case proof will be inadequate.

Now I have told you that emotions also possess an electrical reality. Thoughts formed and sent out within the impulse range of emotion often succeed because of the peculiar nature of the emotional electrical impulses themselves. They have a particularly strong electrical mass. They also usually fall within powerful intensities, for reasons we will not discuss now. Thoughts formed under a strong emotional impetus will carry greater vividness, have a greater tendency toward duplication, and are apt to be interpreted with some success.

Also, all individuals have had familiarity with emotions as they exist within electrical intensities, and are accustomed to reacting to them. The whole process is instantaneous. However, the thought which is now an approximation of the original thought, and actually an identity of its own—that thought is changed once more by the receiver himself. He does not actually interpret the thought itself. He interprets its meaning and forms a new thought identity.

In our last session I told you this. Action, the very action of transmission, alters the nature and electrical reality of the thought itself.

To repeat: our imaginary sender A does not transmit a given thought. He does not even send an exact duplicate. Nor does the receiver receive the thought in the same condition. The original thought is retained by A. A forms a thought as nearly identical as his possibilities allow it to be. This he transmits to B. But B can't receive the thought in its present condition, for the action of receiving a thought also changes it. He forms a thought as nearly identical as possible for him, and interprets it.

Action can never be considered apart from that which is seemingly acted upon, for action becomes part of structure. Action begins from within and is a result of inner vitality inherent in all realities. Action is not a thing alone. It is not an identity. Action is a dimension of existence.

CHAPTER 7

Steps to Psychological Time.

The Light Trance.

Experiments for You; Our Experiments.

The conscious mind is concerned with getting you through daily life. It deals of necessity with time and space. But many experiences which affect us deeply take up no space and seem to exist independently of time as we know it. A deeply felt psychological experience, for example, takes up no space and projects itself through time. Yet such an experience is sometimes more vivid than other realities which we can see and touch.

Our consciousness is usually focused in one direction. We usually look away from our inner selves, toward our outside environment. Most of the time this is an effective method of operation: we must relate ourselves to our physical world for we live in a physical universe. But we are learning that the physical universe itself is basically quite different from the appearance that it presents to our senses. Remember our table, which is not really solid, but only seems to be. We perceive the table as solid, but this does not change the basic nature of the atoms and molecules that compose it.

An idea is every bit as real and practical as a table, for example, but its dimensions differ from those of a physical object. We may speak of an idea as having depth and weight, but we do not mean the same thing as we mean when we say that a river has depth, or an apple has weight. Ideas are also to a large degree independent of time. They are certainly independent of space. Our minds can deal with ideas very well, but our senses cannot perceive them. Though you cannot smell, taste or touch an idea, yet we know that ideas exist and that they are legitimate. Without them no physical advancements would exist, because the ideas for them had to come first.

Ideas come from the inner self, that portion of the self which we so often ignore. Because we focus our energies toward physical objects and their manipulation, we often forget the inner self. This chapter will present experiments for you to try that will allow you to change the focus of your awareness from outer to inner reality, for like ideas and other nonphysical phenomena, extrasensory perceptions also seem to operate independently of space and time.

If our senses allow us to perceive physical reality, they often force us to perceive it in a highly distorted manner. As two-dimensional people would not be aware of a three-dimensional world, and could interpret data from it only through tremendous distortions, so we are largely unaware of reality as it exists undistorted by our own sensual apparatus.

It is very possible that we will never completely understand the physical universe through the use of physical instruments, since the measuring implements themselves are affected by the same distortions that affect the universe. We need another frame of reference, a point somewhat outside our own physical system. Such a point would seem to be the inner self, that part of the self which exists in the same way that an idea exists—within physical matter but independent of it to a large degree.

According to the Seth Material, physical reality is seen as a materialization or construction of mental acts. If so, then systematic investigations into the nature of the inner self and inner abilities should allow us to perceive reality as it exists in a more or less pure form—undistorted by the physical senses.

If all this sounds far-fetched, consider the following. For all our knowledge, man still does not know what the mind is. The physical brain can be probed with instruments. It can be stimulated physically. It is a part of the material universe. Some scientists think that there is no mind as such, that the word "mind" is just a term that refers to the functions of the brain. It is very possible, however, that the mind is simply a part of us that does not appear within physical matter in the same way that ideas or psychological experiences do not appear in physical matter. Joy does not exist as a physical object either, yet no one doubts that joy exists. Dreams are not objects either, yet no one would deny their validity.

The mind would seem to be a part of the inner self that does not wholly appear in physical terms. The brain would be part of the mind, that part which does appear as an object within the body. The mind, then, being apart from physical matter, could serve as the reference point that we need to perceive reality as it exists independently of the distortions given to it by the senses.

In our experiments we will focus inward toward the inner self, for extrasensory perceptions in many cases may well be glimpses of this basic reality. Also since physical time is already known to be artificial, merely a contrived convenience on our part, it is not surprising that extrasensory perceptions tend to act as if time as we know it did not exist. Our idea of time is also distorted, the result of our limited perceptions. It is possible that our conception of time further falsifies our conception of reality.

Is there a way to perceive reality as it exists beneath physical matter's shifting forms? I believe that there is. We can begin by changing the focus of our awareness, and there are many ways of doing this. In dreams, for example, we change the focus of our consciousness easily, and you have seen that extra sensory perceptions appear to show themselves when we are asleep.

Even here, however, there will be some distortions. As the physical senses tend to distort reality while they perceive it, so will the personal subconscious do the same. You can see how this works when you study your own dream notebook and discover valid clairvoyant information mixed in with elements that have nothing to do with the precognitive data at all. By focusing inward, we can rid ourselves of the rigid limitations of the senses, and through experience we can learn to see through the personal subconscious to other realities beyond.

We do not have to be asleep to perceive these realities. We can do just as well and better by adopting a simple trance state where we are partially dissociated from our outer environment. A trance state is merely a condition of increased concentration. It is harmless and can be most beneficial. It can be used as a transition from ordinary wakefulness to what Seth calls "Psychological Time." Psychological Time is a state where your concentration is focused freely inward, in which you experience time as it actually exists.

In the light trance state the inner self is allowed greater freedom. Consciousness is always retained, but outside distractions are ignored. This chapter will show you how to induce this light trance state, how to use it and control it to enrich your life in general and develop your own inner abilities.

In July, 1965, we attended, on invitation, the Hypnosis Symposium III, sponsored jointly by State University College at Oswego, N. Y., and the American Society of Clinical Hypnosis. The symposium was held at the university. One of the important points mentioned was the fact that hypnosis is actually a state of increased concentration, and is not similar to sleep as has erroneously been supposed.

With the aid of hypnosis, the individual is simply able to use native abilities and potentialities of which the ego is not aware. This state of increased concentration can permit us to focus our awareness along desired lines, while we block out distractions. As such it is an excellent tool for the study and development of human personality.

Our own experiments with hypnosis convince us that the hypnotic state is but a variation on the usual state of consciousness. Since individuals often enter a trance state in ordinary life without even being aware of the fact, the trance is certainly a normal aspect of consciousness. It is possible that it has a survival potential which we have not as yet discovered.

The level of consciousness in sleep needs much more study also, as our own investigations make it plain that the personality shows purposeful activity in the dream condition, and that the individual attempts problem solving and other activities that are usually thought to be delegated only to the waking personality.

Hypnosis is merely a method of increasing the powers of concentration. Using self-hypnosis, we can switch gears so to speak, change the focus of our awareness. In this book, however, I suggest self-hypnosis only. Until you are more familiar with the subject in general I do not recommend that you attempt to hypnotize anyone else.

You have been in a light trance many times, probably without even realizing it. When you are concentrating upon one problem to the exclusion of everything else, you are most likely in a light trance state. Often you are in this state when you watch television, and all your attention is directed toward the program you are watching.

Now you can enter the state when you want to, and use it beneficially. There are various methods of achieving this mental condition of concentration. I will describe the way that I have found easiest, most convenient and effective. This trance state will also allow you to relax your physical body whenever you so desire.

First of all, sit in a comfortable chair, or lie down on the bed. Close your eyes. Begin with your feet and relax all your muscles. Speaking aloud or mentally, tell yourself that you will completely relax. Listen to the words in your mind. Suggestion is marvelously effective in inducing relaxation. You will find that you actually are letting down. Progress through all the muscles, going up the calf, thigh, abdominal area, hips, back, up to the waist, through the body to the spinal cord and up the neck.

Imagine the relaxation spreading over the shoulders, down the arms to the elbows and hands and to your fingertips. Then imagine this relaxation spreading up from the neck and shoulders to the throat and jaw, facial muscles, over the brow and scalp. As you continue, you will feel the tension and nervousness leave your body.

In the beginning this process may take about twenty minutes. It may take more or less time depending on your abilities of concentration. Later you will be able to get the same results merely by suggesting to yourself that you can do so. Whenever you use self-hypnosis, be sure to tell yourself that you will snap out of the state whenever you choose, or at the count of three.

It is highly improbable that a trance would last for any degree of time in any case, but the above precaution should always be taken. The only real possibility here is that you might just go off into a natural sleep. For this reason it is a good policy to tell yourself that you will not fall off to sleep. Your physical body will be very relaxed, however, and if you do doze off the first few times, do not be discouraged. You will soon learn the knack of maintaining the proper state. In this condition your mind is very alert and concentration is of a high level. Your body will be relaxed and your mind will be free of physical distractions.

You may even doubt that you are in a light trance state, since sometimes there is little noticeable difference in the feel of your awareness. There is, however, a subtle change in your conscious relationship with the physical environment. Your eyes are closed. You know that the room is there. Sounds may rush up from the street. The difference is that you are no longer interested or concerned with such stimuli.

If you want to prove to yourself that you are in a trance state, you may do so. In the beginning this may be good for your self-confidence. Later you will be able to tell, simply by the feel of your own consciousness. Here is a test that you can use. With your eyes closed, and after you have brought yourself to a relaxed condition through suggestion, tell yourself that you cannot open your eyes. Tell yourself firmly that the harder you try to open your eyes the tighter closed they will become.

Repeat this several times. Then try to open your eyes. To your surprise, you will discover that you cannot do so.

As soon as you have assured yourself in this manner that you are in the trance state, then at once remove the suggestion. Suggest that you can now open your eyes if you want to, but do not open them as this might return you to normal consciousness.

Or you may try this test instead. After you have relaxed yourself, tell yourself that strength and power are flowing through your right arm. If you are left-handed, use the left arm for this test. Hold the arm out in the air and repeat the suggestion firmly. Tell yourself that the arm is growing rigid, stiff as a board. Suggest that you cannot bend the arm at all, and that the harder you try to bend the arm the stiffer it will become. Then try to bend the arm. You will find that you cannot bend it. It will indeed seem stiff as a piece of board and will move only as a whole unit. Then immediately remove the suggestions. Tell yourself that the arm is now relaxed and mobile, and can be flexed. The arm will then return to its normal state.

I am including these tests only so that you can prove to yourself that you are in a light trance state if you choose to do so. They are not necessary for our purposes. If you do use either test, be certain that you remove the prohibitive suggestions as soon as you have completed the test.

When you are finished with the relaxation technique, simply sit or lie quietly. Do not make any further suggestions at this point except to tell yourself that you are filled with vitality and health. The state of relaxation which you will have achieved is beneficial from a variety of viewpoints. The nervousness which affects most of us is effectively banished in the light trance state. I have used the light trance most effectively to reduce discomfort and pain when visiting the dentist.

In this book we will be concerned with the trance in its relationship to the ego, however. For in this mental condition we are able to step aside to some degree from the ego, which is always so concerned with physical environment. We are able to concentrate upon the inner self and momentarily forget the self which is involved with daily chores.

I would suggest that you remain in the trance state no longer than fifteen minutes to begin with. You may suggest that your own subconscious will snap you out of the trance and it will do so. Or you may set the alarm clock. Fifteen minutes allows you sufficient time to acclimate yourself to the new conditions of your consciousness. Later you can allow yourself more time if you prefer.

In the trance state your conception of time is different from what it usually is. The inner self is free from clock time in the same manner as it is when you are dreaming. In a daydream, for example, you may feel that no clock time at all has passed, only to "wake up" and discover that an hour has gone by. It is possible that more time will pass than you realize when you are in the trance state also.

You can also achieve this relaxed state however without using self-hypnosis. Simply lie or sit quietly. Try the experiment listed in the chapter on telepathy, in which you recognize your own stream of consciousness and then ignore it. Mentally explore the darkness behind your closed eyelids. With practice you will be able to focus your awareness inward rather than outward.

Now what can you expect in this state? How can you actually learn to recognize and use your own inner abilities? First of all you will have dissociated yourself to some degree from physical environment. You will be conscious of it; you will know that it is there; but you will be able to ignore it. You will probably experience a most pleasant feeling of detachment. Sounds may appear louder for a short while, but then you will hardly notice them.

Then, simply concentrate your awareness within your own inner self. You may, as in earlier experiments, hear voices or words or see images. These may originate within the personal subconscious, or they may come from deeper layers of the self, portions of the self that can perceive reality through other means than the physical senses. You must write down what you see or hear immediately after each experiment. Often you may recognize mental events suddenly, only to realize that they have been happening for quite some time without your being aware of them. In fact, often you will have to learn to give them durability yourself.

I will recount here some of our own experiences with this state of dissociation, including both significant and relatively insignificant incidents. Here is a rather simple but interesting experience that happened about five months after we had begun experimenting.

Robert is an artist. He had been awarded a portrait prize at the local art gallery and on the evening involved we were to attend a reception at which the awards would be announced. After dinner I put myself in a light trance state. It was 6 P.M. and I wanted to begin dressing by 7. It had been a busy day. I dozed, lost all conception of time, and woke suddenly with my eyes still closed. "I wonder what time it is?" I thought. Instantly behind my closed eyelids I saw clearly the clock that was in Robert's studio. Even if my eyes had been opened, and they weren't, I couldn't have seen that particular clock from my bed. There was no clock at all in the room in which I was resting. I saw the time easily: ten minutes before seven. I accepted this, almost without thinking about it, and instructed my subconscious to let me doze for ten more minutes. When I awakened again I immediately called to Robert, asking him what time it was. It was seven o'clock.

The following incident is much more startling. It happened in the morning, while I was in a light trance state. The experience itself was initiated by an unusual sensation which will be discussed in the next chapter. I felt a quick inner jolt about my head and instantly found myself standing in front of the house in which I grew up. There was no transition at all.

One moment I was conscious of the bed beneath my body, and the next instant I felt my feet upon a snowy sidewalk. The experience was so clear and vivid, so real, that I had a sudden sense of disorientation. Was I dreaming? Was this a hallucination? I looked about. The houses looked ordinary. They were the houses I remembered. I knew that it was April. But then, where did the snow come from? How did I get from Elmira to Saratoga Springs, and arrive in the middle of winter? The trees were bare of foliage. I knew the neighborhood well, though I had not been home in years. My family no longer lived in the house before which I was standing. Then something odd caught my eye: the last time I had visited Saratoga, the house across the street from my old home had been enclosed with a fence. There was no fence there now, and no hint that one had ever been there.

Where was the fence? I tried to figure out what had happened. I wasn't frightened, only astonished. Just then three boys came up the road. They dragged a sled behind them. Instantly I recognized one of the boys as being an old friend, D. H. About to call out to him, I stopped in confusion: D. H. is ten years younger than myself. He would be a grown man. There was no mistake. I looked again. The boy was clearly D. H. as a child. With this realization, I felt myself begin to leave the scene. It did not seem to disappear, but it was as if I were withdrawing from it. How, I don't know, but I managed to bring myself back to it. This time I stood there, taking stock for some moments.

The boys were already disappearing, taking a short cut that I knew well. "Of course," I thought. "D. H.'s mother lives around the corner, I can visit her any time I like." Then I remembered that I had not seen D. H.'s mother in ten years. At the same time, another thought occurred to me. This was the street exactly as it had been in the past! The fence across the way had not been erected yet! Suddenly I was back in bed again. I felt the pillows beneath my head. Opening my eyes, I looked about my familiar bedroom. The street and the houses were gone.

Now age regression, or the psychological return of an individual to a past event, is a phenomenon that is not at all unusual under hypnosis. One such experience will convince anyone that the personal subconscious contains complete and detailed memories of all our experiences, and can, under certain circumstances, allow us to relive them. This is not a process of remembering. It involves an actual reliving of the event itself within a psychological framework.

The experience just related could be a very vivid regression to a particular incident which I have consciously forgotten. But to me there is no doubt that, for all practical purposes, I had left my own bedroom. My senses no longer perceived it. I cannot prove that my body was still on the bed while I was somewhere else, over 200 miles away in space and fifteen years or so away in time. Nor could I prove that my body was not on the bed. Wherever my body was for those moments, I do know that the essential part of myself was in Saratoga Springs, N.Y. My feet were cold from the snow. I was myself, my own age, using all my faculties to discover the nature of the situation in which I found myself.

This could have been age regression. It could have been an experience in what is called astral projection. I do not myself think that age regression was involved; perhaps because the peculiar physical sensation that initiated the experience is usually not connected with age regression. And this physical sensation has been involved with other such experiences on my part. Much more investigation is needed along these lines. There are too many questions not answered, and too many questions not even being asked.

If you should have a similar experience, speak to whoever you see. Try to establish contact. This was the first such incident in which I was involved. Not until later did I regret that I had not called out to D. H. There was nothing to prevent me from trying to pick up a handful of snow; or walking across the street. Yet at the time I did not think of these things.

It goes without saying that the scene was as real to me as the familiar scene outside my window. The experience was as much a part of my reality as any of the other more ordinary experiences of that particular day. It was as much an event as the event of my lunch which followed shortly after. But was the incident also real in physical terms? Did it exist, perhaps, in a different space-time continuum? Such questions are quite legitimate. It is very possible that our ideas of reality are severely limited. Even the type of questions that we ask are determined by what we believe to be possible and not possible. And our questions limit our investigations and determine their nature.

But the experience just mentioned, and the following one which happened to Robert, occurred during the early phases of our experiments. We have both had others. Robert put himself into a light trance state. He was in bed. Without transition of any kind, he found himself standing in an office building on 57th Street in New York City. He recognized it as one in which he had done business in the past. Now he stood in a hallway.

To his left was a narrow window of vertical design, with an aluminum or stainless steel frame. Looking out of this window, he saw a shining steel guard rail. Beneath this was a stone parapet, some ten feet below. A girl stood in front of him, between him and the window. She was trying to open the window, which was designed to swing inward, in two sections, with an upper and lower half.

The girl had long black hair. She was slim, and wore a yellow sleeveless silky blouse. Afterward Robert couldn't remember the color of her skirt, though at the time he saw it clearly. He thought of helping her open the window, when suddenly he was back in bed. The office building and the girl were gone.

This incident, like the one that happened to me, had as much reality as any other event that occurred during the same day. In fact, such incidents have more reality, in a way, since they are so unusual. If this was a hallucination, it was a particularly vivid one. Robert felt as if he stood in the building as it existed in present, rather than past, time. The girl, the building, and all the details had solidity, or at least they certainly appeared solid and real in physical terms.

As far as your own experiments are concerned, try to check as many facts as you can. In the following chapter we will be concerned with an experience such as this where Robert did attempt to make contact. If you seem to be in a friend's house, by all means try to talk to him if you see him. Then, later, check with your friend through ordinary methods of communication. Unfortunately, so far our experiences of this type have not involved friends.

We simply do not know enough about the nature of reality, for instance, to take it for granted that such a friend would not see or hear you under the circumstances. We do not know if the inner self has some sort of electrical reality which can be made visible or not. If your friend could not see you with his eyes, perhaps you would be visible under such conditions to someone else who would perceive you on a different basis.

As you progress with your own experiments, you may discover that you are suddenly aware of an experience only to realize that it has been going on for some time, but you were not aware of it. In the beginning, your ego may clamp down, so that the words or images disappear. Practice will allow you to increase the durability of such instances. There seems to be some kind of subconscious mechanism involved here. When you reach a certain level of consciousness it is as if your awareness is released and your consciousness is freed momentarily from its focus upon physical reality.

Do not become so involved with the mechanics of the light trance that you forget to use it merely as a tool to increase your own concentration. Do not keep wondering how far "under" you are, or whether or not the session will be productive. This will only defeat your purpose. All sessions will not involve images or words or definite experiences of any sort. You will, however, learn how to deal with your inner self and, in this respect, all sessions will be productive.

The dissociation of the consciousness from physical environment is what we are concerned with, and with the increased concentration that this makes possible. Then we want to turn this concentration inward. It does not matter whether you achieve this state by using self-hypnosis or the other method here suggested. Anyone who is used to focusing his energies upon one task to the exclusion of others has reached this state often.

When each experiment is over, write down what happened at once. Whatever you see or hear must be faithfully recorded. On those occasions when you have vivid experiences, you will know it. Others may be less vivid and you will forget them if they are not recorded in your notes. It is difficult to describe subjective states of mind, but you should make every effort to do so.

This light trance state, or this condition of increased concentration, can also be useful in connection with other experiments. Sometime when you are in the light trance, tell yourself that you will be able to open your eyes and still stay under hypnosis. This suggestion is necessary as there is a tendency to come out of the trance, at this level, if the eyes are opened. Then run through your ESP cards. You may find that your score is higher when you are able to concentrate in this manner. Make sure that on your record sheets you add the fact that the test was done while in the trance state.

If you have tried automatic writing with little or no success in the past, then when you are in a trance suggest that you will now be able to write automatically. Have a large sheet of paper nearby and a soft, dark pencil. Tell yourself that your subconscious mind will utilize your hand to write on any subject that it so chooses. Write your name at the top of the page. Reread what was already said in an earlier chapter concerning automatic writing, and follow those directions while you are in a state of increased concentration.

If you are using self-hypnosis, I recommend only the induction method that I have given in this book. Looking into crystal balls, watching pendulums and the like can induce the trance state rather quickly, before you have realized what has happened. For this reason I strongly discourage erratic experimentation with such methods.

The following are excerpts from the Seth sessions that deal with subject matter that we have covered in this chapter. The first excerpt is from session 14. It goes without saying that only small portions of the material can be given in this book, but all the subjects mentioned are discussed thoroughly and in full in the body of the material.

Everything on your plane is a materialization of something that exists independent of your plane. Therefore within your senses there are other senses that perceive inward. Your regular senses perceive, or create, an outer world. The senses within perceive and create an inner world. They perceive part of an inner world.

It is almost as if you could feel, touch and perceive so much outwardly and feel, touch and perceive so much inwardly, though much exists in all directions of which you are necessarily ignorant. Once you exist within a particular field, you must be attuned to it while blocking out many other perceptions.

It is a sort of psychic focus, a concentration of awareness along certain lines. As your ability grows in relation with the environment on your plane, you then can afford to look around, use the inner senses and enlarge your scope of activity. This is only natural. Survival on a particular plane or within a particular field depends upon your concentration in that plane. When survival is more or less satisfied, then you can turn your attention elsewhere.

From Session 25

Much investigation along the lines of ESP is being carried on within the western world. The fact is that western man has not only cut himself off from half of his own ability and half of his knowledge because of his insistence upon an artificial dual nature, but he has also cut himself off from the very primitive societies from which he could learn much about his abilities.

His education, his everyday pattern of existence, his cultural values, tend to imprison him so that he can view other societies only through the murky maze of his own misconceptions. If he considers a native in Africa, for example, as a superstitious, rather imbecilic, almost prehistoric creature from the past, then he will learn nothing of that man's abilities. He will ridicule any such evidence of so-called ESP on the native's part as further proof of the African's childlike mind.

The fact remains that psychologists or scientists cannot speak of ESP as either below normal or above normal as far as the species is concerned, just because western man finds such difficulty in using it with any effectiveness. Other peoples manage to use it in a rather effective manner.

The trouble with ESP investigations is that you are using the wrong tools. You are taking this dual self for granted again. Until you realize that there is one self, and not one self who does and manipulates and another self who breathes and dreams, you will get nowhere. Investigations carried on according to what are considered scientific precepts are doomed in a large measure to slow motion tactics at best, and to complete failure at worst.

This does not mean that evidence cannot be found, and overwhelming evidence, for the existence of the inner senses. It does mean that spontaneity must be allowed for. It is extremely difficult to relate data received by the inner senses to data that will be picked up by the outer senses.

Again, you get something like a mirror image that must be deciphered. Data received by the inner senses will have its own discernible impact upon the personality receiving it, and this impact is as strong as any impact caused by outer stimuli.

When you insist upon evidence through the regularly accepted senses, you almost automatically turn off the inner sense apparatus. This is not necessary. Man has set up this reaction himself to a large degree. You must take the inner data at its face value, and this is what you will not do. Once you take this first step of spontaneity, you will actually receive evidence that even the conscious mind will be forced to accept. But the first step of such willingness must be made.

If you once allow yourself freely to receive inner data in a spontaneous, non-critical manner, you will see that this data is as legitimate, valid and varied, and as powerful as any outside stimuli. But to insist upon translating this data into channels that can *first* be picked up by the outer senses, and then expect strong undistorted data, is impossible.

The impressions received by the inner senses are, again, actually concrete in a way that you do not now understand. This data also has physical effects upon the brain. In the same manner that impressions received from outside stimuli affect the brain, they make their effect upon it. They change the personality as any experience does. To insist upon evidence in terms of outside sensual data is as ridiculous a notion as to expect a camera to play music.

Music exists and can be played on a phonograph. Sights can be captured on a camera. But you do not expect music to come from a camera. You do not expect a phonograph to take pictures. Yet you are expecting the outer senses to do something that they are not capable of doing. You are expecting them to act like a camera that can pick up music. . . . At the same time you are refusing to use the very inner senses which are equipped to handle the data that you wish to capture.

It is your refusal to accept the whole self that causes the difficulty. Once more: data received by the inner senses are as vivid, and in fact more vivid, than any other data you will ever receive. The ironic part of the whole matter is that you actually receive this inner data constantly. You utilize it constantly, and yet consciously you will not admit its existence.

The very fact that you breathe and dream and perform countless other activities without any aid from the conscious ego should convince the most stubborn skull that more is involved here than science is willing to admit. Your present idea of the subconscious is merely a grudging, hedging, partial admission that man is more than his conscious ego, more than the sum of his parts, and more than a mechanism.

Evidence of what you call ESP will be arrived at, but as you receive evidence of sound through the ears and do not ordinarily expect to see through your ears, so evidence must come through the correct channels. One of your main difficulties is that you will not accept as evidence anything which is not perceivable in one manner or other through the outer senses. That is, you will not consider an experience as valid unless it can be demonstrated to exist as physical camouflage reality.

Almost everyone is familiar with something else, however, and that is psychological experience which may have no observable physical effect and yet can change a personality to a large degree. . . .

[Examples follow here. Since I have used some of this material already in this chapter, this section will not be quoted.]

[Data received by the inner] senses are as intense and sometimes more so than any psychological experience. And, as I said earlier, you cannot hold a psychological experience in your hands and examine it either. Nor examine it in a laboratory. But the worst of fools would not deny psychological experiences for this reason.

The term ESP is itself a result of your artificial duality, maintaining as it does that anything not perceived through the physical senses is therefore extra and tacked on. . . . It must be admitted that the outside senses are fabricators of the most delightful sort. What will you do when you discover that everything the physical senses tell you is, in a basic manner, false?

On the other hand, the inner senses are more reliable. Your inner data are more reliable. Your psychological experience is valid whether chairs are solid or not. [This refers to an earlier statement.] Inner data, and the inner self which you deny, are a lot more permanent, and I am speaking to you as proof.

CHAPTER 8

Psychological Time.

More about Trance States.

Experiments for You; Our Experiments.

Characteristics of Consciousness.

There is very little known about the characteristics of consciousness at any level. Consciousness certainly varies in degree. Sometimes we are more conscious than at other times, and the focus of our awareness seems more intense. We have a sense of being more alive than usual when we are under the stimulus of a strong emotion such as love or hate. On occasion an emotion is so powerful that it seems to sweep us away. We forget ourselves for a moment. When this happens and the egotistical *I* is carried away, then what part of us is it that experiences heightened consciousness?

In our ordinary conscious state we are not aware of all aspects of ourselves or our environment by any means. We are, however, usually fairly attentive to physical stimuli. We listen to what others say. We do not listen inward, with our ears, to our own heartbeat. Our senses orient us to the material world. They are directed outward. Our eyes look at objects and other people. They do not look inward, organically speaking. Our ordinary state of consciousness, therefore, can be characterized as outgoing. The part of us that is so engrossed with objects and physical environment is the ego. It thinks and reasons, looks outward, and interprets what it sees.

Is this then the limit of our consciousness? Hardly. If

so, we would always be completely unconscious in sleep, with no dreams. Each night would be a nothingness with no flashes of identity. If the ego were the only conscious part of us, then, when the ego slept, each sleep would be a small death, with no dream memories at all. On awakening we would have no assurance whatsoever that we had existed as ourselves during the night.

Our ordinary state of consciousness is also characterized by a regulating sense of time. But all states of consciousness are not so characterized. You can probably remember countless occasions when you forgot time—and while you were wide awake. During some instances you were most likely so wrapped up in what was happening that you forgot yourself. What you forgot, again, was the ego, the egotistical *I,* who is so concerned with the measurement of time. Yet you were certainly conscious.

The ego attempts to stand apart from all the rest of reality. But when we are under the influence of a strong emotion, we forget to stand apart. We forget the ego. We almost become what it is we feel. We experience reality directly, so directly that such an experience can be unsettling. We feel that we have lost control, as when we give way to anger. Yet when we give way to joy we do not feel that we have lost control, but gained freedom. In either case, the ego is momentarily pushed aside while we experience vivid emotions. The result, oddly enough, is heightened consciousness.

Those of you who enjoy dancing will know what I mean. When you let yourself go, give in to the music, you find yourself dancing far better than you would if you held back. You are in a state of heightened consciousness often when you dance in such a manner. Your body seems to perform the dance on its own. You are much too engrossed in dancing to consider time or to be aware of the self who dances. You may also be in a trance state—a period of heightened concentration—and one that is generally accepted by society and yourself.

The state of your consciousness as you dance is quite different from what it was earlier, as you prepared to go out for the evening. First of all, while dancing you experience a feeling of freedom. But freedom from what or for what? Freedom from the separation of your own feelings. For the ego always separates you from what you feel to some degree. Otherwise, you would have no protection from anger and hatred, and from your own reactions to them. But in so protecting you, the ego also denies you the full experience of joy or love, and so sets up barriers that you do not need. An ego that is too rigid will prevent full appreciation of any emotion and make life very drab indeed.

It is necessary that we teach the ego to be flexible, so that it can give us necessary support and still allow us freedom. For as the ego sets up barriers between ourselves and our emotions, it also limits our consciousness in other areas. It refuses to accept perceptions that are not part of its own idea of reality.

This is due in part to our educational system. We educate intuition out of our children. We teach them that reality lies outside themselves entirely. We discourage any perceptions from within unless they are immediately practical in physical terms. Our own conception of reality is severely limited as a result. We have trained our egos too well.

We can remedy the situation. We can slowly teach the ego to accept inner experiences, while still retaining its regulatory functions. We can, quite simply, start looking inward. We can turn our attention from physical reality now and then and freely explore the inner environment, the inner self. We can learn to concentrate or focus our awareness within ourselves and discover the full potentialities that lie within the self.

We can perceive portions of that reality which exists independently of the appearance given to it by our own physical senses, and allow ourselves to become aware of extrasensory perceptions that are usually blocked by the ego. To do this, we must achieve a greater freedom than we have previously allowed ourselves.

Such intense concentration can be called a deep trance state. Do not let the term confuse you, however. We are merely speaking of various directions in which conscious-

ness can turn. You need not even use self-hypnosis if
you prefer not to do so. What we are concerned with is
inward concentration. We want to look away from physical objects for a change. The terms used make no difference to the basic experience, or to the results.

For that matter, our state of everyday consciousness
can also be considered as a trance. We are caught up in
physical reality to the exclusion of everything else. All our
attention is captured. We are more intently concentrated
in the world of everyday life than we can ever be when
we attempt to turn our awareness inward toward psychological and mental phenomena. We are so transfixed by
physical reality that we are afraid to turn our eyes away
for a moment, as if it would not be there when we got
back.

Yet that very physical universe is dependent upon the
inner state of our being. Our ideas and intuitions must
exist first, before they can be made practical and given
objective existence. Those of you who are adventurous
and also reasonable, who are intuitive and also logical,
who are curious and also cautious, can learn much by
learning to switch your awareness from outer to inner
reality.

By this time, through your own experiments, you
should have convinced yourself of the existence of extrasensory perceptions in general. You should have recognized some instances of it in your own dreams if you
followed my instructions. Your ego has already expanded
to some degree. It is less rigid, more flexible. Perhaps you
are ready now to go a step further.

A very brief review is needed here. Let me repeat again
that our physical senses do distort the nature of reality,
and actually limit our perception of it to some considerable degree. If there is an "objective reality" independent
of the perceiver, then I do not believe it is a reality of
physical matter.

The inner self is not limited in its perception by the
senses. It can perceive this basic reality and it is possible
that extrasensory perceptions are but glimpses of it. We
can change the focus of our awareness and so enable

ourselves to become conscious of realities that are not accessible to the senses. Telepathy, clairvoyance and precognitive dreams may be only aspects of a larger perceptive ability that lies inherent within the human personality.

In this chapter we will consider the ways in which we can turn our attention inward in order to enlarge the scope of consciousness. The experiments require self-discipline and common sense. They do not require specialized training or education. They do require objectivity, psychological balance, intuition and a sense of wonder, but every worthwhile endeavor calls for these specifications. An exploration into inner reality demands most of all the courage to look into yourself, into aspects of your own consciousness you have ignored in the past.

First of all, we believe extrasensory perceptions happen by themselves under certain conditions. We do not know all of those conditions, but we do know some of them. These perceptions often appear when we are under the influence of some powerful emotion, or when we are completely relaxed and receptive, and the conscious mind is directed elsewhere. In other words, ESP often shows itself when we are not concerned with the ego. When we are emotionally excited the ego lets go to some extent. When we are relaxed, it also eases its hold and is not geared for action.

Since we want to develop our abilities, we will try to bring about this natural spontaneous state of inner freedom on purpose for use as needed. We will try to do this not by stirring up our emotions, though this is one less efficient way, but by relaxing the ego and turning our attention inward.

Those of you who are using self-hypnosis may induce a light trance state as earlier suggested. Then assure yourself you can deepen the trance and give full concentration to inner reality. Repeat this several times. Always tell yourself you will snap out of the trance state whenever you choose, at the count of three, or within a specific period of time. Again, the only possibility here is that you might fall off to a natural sleep. Suggest that you are now able to extend your consciousness and expand it. Then make no further suggestions.

Those of you who are using simple relaxation rather than self-hypnosis should simply relax completely as in earlier exercises. Be lax and receptive but at the same time turn the focus of your consciousness inward. Be mentally alert but quiet. Make your mind a blank. This simply means that the ego is not filling it with its own thoughts. There are no limitations to your own inner awareness. There are no real limitations to the self basically, though we act as if there were for practical reasons. Try and feel your relationship with the universe as you know it. Don't think about, but feel, whatever you experience while you are trying this experiment.

Regardless of which method you are using, you should attain a more intense inner concentration than you did for the experiments listed in the preceding chapters. There may be an almost complete absence of the sense of passing time. The experiences of which you are aware may seem to exist in a dimension of their own. You may feel a physical lightness. You may see some images so clearly that you think your eyes are open. The first few times that this happens you will probably be tempted to open them, as I was. Later you will take the vividness of such images for granted when they do occur.

Ordinarily when you close your eyes, there is darkness behind the lids. When you are concentrating inward, however, the usual dark area may suddenly be filled with light as bright or brighter than daylight. It may last a while or it may merely flash spasmodically. You may think that the sun has just come out if it is a dark day, or that someone has turned the light on in the room. Sometimes you may experience a feeling of vibration.

Seth calls this condition of increased inward concentration a state of Psychological Time in which awareness is free from the usual physical limitations put upon it. Clock time as we know it is no longer a reality. Clock time is a reality that must be manipulated by the ego. It becomes nonexistent for all practical purposes when we bypass the ego to any considerable degree.

Some very definite physical sensations in my case seem to serve as signals for extrasensory perceptions under these conditions. Robert does not experience these particular sensations, so it does not seem as if they are conditions necessary for extrasensory perceptiveness in general.

The most vivid of my experiences have always been preceded by such feelings. A kinetic sense of being quickly tapped on the head initiates such "traveling" incidents as the one related earlier in this book. The sensation is definite. Once my head wobbled back and forth, the tap was so sharp. Yet no pain was ever involved. I did not actually believe anyone was hitting me on the head. Nor did I have bumps to show! Sound is also connected with this. The only thing I could compare it to would be the inner sound that might accompany a chiropractic adjustment of some severity.

For me a very loud static seems to precede experiences which have to do with sound in general, such as those in which voices are involved. Here is an example from my records of such an incident. I will quote the entry exactly as it was written, immediately after the experience, since it is rather difficult to paraphrase.

"I lay down to try Psychological Time. Suddenly from the living room came the sound of static. It was quite loud and unmistakable. There was a voicelike sound in it also. I was tempted to get up and see if I had left the radio playing but I was certain it was turned off. Then I recalled that the same sort of thing happened last week. I heard static, and then orchestration. Yet when I checked, I found that the radio was off. We never play television in the day, but I checked to be certain and the set was also turned off. The orchestration continued. It did not seem to come from outside my head that time, but it was definite. So when I heard the static today I did not get up, but continued with my Psychological Time experiment.

"I put myself into a light trance state. Then, on impulse, I asked mentally, 'What was wrong with L. G.'s neck?' [Visiting a friend the night before, L. G. had complained of discomfort in his throat.] Instantly I heard the following in a loud, impatient voice: 'What do you mean, neck? It's a bad tongue that's causing the trouble!'

"It seemed that I picked the words up with my ears from my outside environment. They did not seem this time to come within my head. It was as if a radio had suddenly been turned on, excessively loud, right beside me. There was that static, booming, and the loud voice. The voice was a man's, heavy and exasperated. I jumped as anyone will do when a sudden noise sounds beside them. Instantly I opened my eyes. I was alone. Remembering the earlier static, I rushed to check the radio and television. They were both turned off."

Unfortunately L.G. does not live in this city. It was over a month before we saw him again. His throat no longer troubled him. He had not seen a doctor. There was no way of knowing whether or not a tongue condition had caused his difficulty. This experience is one of several in which the static preceded the incident, and also formed the background of the event itself. Sometimes the static becomes kinetic in that it seems to originate within myself. In some odd manner it is then mixed with actual physical sensation.

Robert and I have both been subjectively certain that we left our physical images during some of our experiments with Psychological Time. Robert once felt himself rise up from his body through the chest region. Until more experimentation is conducted, such subjective experiences raise more questions than they answer. All in all, a sense of freedom and well-being, plus an absence of a time sense, probably characterizes Psychological Time more than such unusual incidents do.

Some of these experiments caused us to believe the astral body idea is not so far-fetched as it might first appear. Robert has been subjectively convinced that his arms were crossed on his chest, when he knew that his physical arms lay at his sides. He has, from a corner of the room, looked back at his own physical image. On at least one occasion, I felt as if I were leaving my image, resisted, and did not do so.

The tap-on-the-head sensation warns me that something unusual is about to happen, and this leads to an interesting question. Is it possible that these signaling sensations may be warning devices set up by my own ego, rather than sensations that trigger such experiences?

There is also another characteristic that seems to be a part of Psychological Time consciousness. We call this ecstasy, though we dislike the term. It is a definite thrilling sensation, quite vivid, accompanied sometimes by a feeling of weightlessness and an expansion of consciousness. It varies in degree from a generalized pleasantness which is stronger than any usual sense of well-being, to a definite feeling of joy and oneness with reality as a whole.

It is all too easy to label such experiences hallucinations, or to say that they are simply the results of suggestion or overworked imaginations. For one thing, we do not know enough about hallucinations nor suggestion. They are only words describing experiences into which we have refused to look very deeply. It is known that under certain conditions blisters can be made to form on human flesh as a result of suggestion. I have myself made headaches disappear within minutes after they began to bother me, through suggestion. Though I cannot prove the next statement scientifically, since the situation was far from scientific, I am convinced that I stopped blisters from forming on my hand, after a severe burn, through suggestion. Suggestion must be of more powerful and substantial nature than is generally supposed, if it can have such effects upon the human physical system.

It is also highly ridiculous to call hallucinations unreal. They may have no physical reality. This does not mean that they do not have reality within dimensions that are quite as legitimate and quite as "real." They may seem to be distortions of physical reality but physical reality itself is highly distorted by the senses. It is even possible that hallucinations in some cases approach nearer to basic reality than we realize.

It might also be recalled here that Christian philosophy as well as Oriental thought has long maintained the existence of a self or soul that was basically independent of physical matter. Under the circumstances it would seem that religion would have much to gain and little to lose by carrying out its own investigations. Perhaps it could prove as facts many ideas which it has never attempted to test on any logical basis.

Occasionally it is considered a mark of sophistication to scoff at the possibility of astral bodies, clairvoyance, telepathy or extrasensory perceptions in general; but while it is true that neurotics are sometimes drawn to such interests, it is also true that extensive investigations of this nature require self-discipline and objectivity and persistence—abilities usually lacking in neurotic temperaments. Nor is the field of psychic phenomena the only field by any means which attracts unbalanced personalities. Religion, the arts, politics and psychology are only a few of the areas to which neurotics flock.

The label "superstitious" is also sometimes tagged to psychic investigation in general. Let it be remembered that medical science is now discovering newer wonder drugs all the time, many of them based on the "superstitious" beliefs of the past. Physics is also coming rather close to old ideas concerning the undependable nature of physical reality.

Baseless superstitions do exist. Some neurotics are apt to be gullible. But all superstitions are not baseless, and all neurotics are not gullible nor drawn to quack theories. This sort of reasoning involves us in a sort of unfortunate guilt by association logic, which prevents many qualified men from working in the field of psychic phenomena.

For that matter, many writers and artists are neurotic, but very few people seriously question the legitimate nature of literature or art. Many neurotic personalities have contributed much to human knowledge in their own fields of endeavor; but in the area of ESP, as in other areas, we must keep open minds and evaluate theories and hypotheses on the basis of their possible validity, and not on other more emotional considerations.

There are, however, many questions involving psychic phenomena that must be answered, and many questions that are still waiting to be asked. Some experiences can be checked out, and their validity proven to all but those whose preconceptions continuously cause them to block new ideas. Other experiences are, or seem, impossible to check in any real manner even while they are evocative enough to suggest that more than subconscious prefabrication is involved.

The following experience of Robert's is one such incident. It took place during a Psychological Time experiment and the following is quoted directly from the account he wrote in his notebook:

"Suddenly I was directly above a parked car, an older type of rounded gray sedan. I was looking down on the top of this old car, and at a wiry, youngish man in a white shirt, sleeves of which were rolled up to his elbows. He circled the car quickly as I watched.

" 'Say,' I said, 'What's going on down there?'

"He looked up at me. He appeared to see me all right and he did not seem surprised. He pointed to the car. 'There's a man in there,' he said. 'Something's terribly wrong with him.'

"The man with whom I was speaking had thick brown hair and slim, muscular build, a wide generous mouth and a squarish jaw. Now he appeared very worried. As he spoke to me I seemed to see him all alone on a screen, cut off at the waist by the screen itself. The rest of the screen was blank, and his figure was rather small in relation to the size of it. Each time he spoke, he seemed to lean forward into the screen from the lower right.

" 'Can you see me?' I said.

" 'Oh sure, I can see you,' he said.

" 'What is your name?'

" 'My name is George Marshall,' he said.

" 'What town is this? Where do you live?' I asked.

"He gave a clear answer, but I could not remember the name of the town, only the name of the state, which was Louisiana. Somehow I thought that we were in the northeast corner of the state. Things began to get hazy, as if I were having trouble focusing on the situation. Almost desperately I said, 'My name is Robert Butts. I live in Elmira. Will you write to me?' I do not recall giving my street address. The man said he would try to contact me."

In this experience, Robert was very conscious of the importance of trying to establish contact with the man involved. We have never heard from George Marshall, however. Robert was not asleep. This was a waking event. Later Robert looked at the map, hoping to come across the name of a city in Louisiana that would jog his memory. There were several towns in the northeast corner of the state whose names sounded familiar, but nothing definite came of this. He couldn't remember the name of the town or city no matter how hard he tried.

It is possible that the incident was subconscious fabrication, but neither of us believe it was. It is also possible that Robert actually did see a man called George Marshall—a George Marshall who also did not remember many of the pertinent parts of the conversation because of the circumstances.

Until such a man can be proven to exist, a man with the same name, a man who could give evidence that he stood beside such a car on the precise day in question, then we cannot say that the experience was definitely extrasensory. By the same token, however, no one can prove that a George Marshall was not in that particular situation on that particular day, standing by an old car in which a man was ill. Neither can it be proven, therefore, that the experience was not a legitimate one in which extrasensory perception was involved.

In all such cases Robert and I constantly try to establish contact when possible. The trouble is you are never prepared as well as you might be because the experiences do not happen that often, and you never know when they will occur. Such data could do much to prove beyond doubt the validity of such experiences.

Not too many years ago a man who spoke of seeing another man on a screen connected to a box in his living room would have been considered quite mad. A century or so ago he might have been burned at the stake. Yet millions watch whole plays today on the television screen. Had such a thing been considered impossible by all men, we would not have television now. Early attempts in many fields were scoffed at by men whose grandchildren enjoy the fruits of those endeavors.

Robert saw a man on a screen and spoke to him. Can the possibility of such contact really be considered so outlandish in a world where two-way television is a reality? Only the box was missing. Investigations in the field of extrasensory perception, unsophisticated as they may be, might very well result in knowledge that will enable mankind to use and understand abilities of which it has largely been ignorant. In some distant future we may be able to utilize these potentials for the benefit of all. It will help us also if we consider again our use of electricity and light waves. We find them very practical, but even the scientists do not really know what electricity is nor what light waves are.

As far as your own experiments are concerned, it is much better to put them on some sort of a regular basis when this is possible. Spasmodic, overly enthusiastic attempts will not yield good results, and the discipline involved in scheduled experiments may also be beneficial. If you are using self-hypnotism, always give the suggestion that you will snap out of the trance state whenever you want to, at the count of three, or within a specified time limit. Under no circumstances do I recommend taking more than a half hour for any of these experiments which involve a change of focus.

Keep your notebook. Immediately after each experiment, make your entry. Compare the contents of your notebook with your dream notebook. See if there is a relation between your dreams and your Psychological Time experiences.

Do not expect spectacular results. You may achieve them—sometimes—but often your Psychological Time experiments will simply involve a sense of well-being and health. Many of our own sessions are uneventful. Each session will increase your own ability to recognize inner experience, and help acclimate you to the "timeless" quality that so characterizes it.

Following are excerpts from the Seth Material in which

some topics are discussed that have a bearing on the subject matter in this chapter.

Excerpts from Session 162

A thought is an action. A dream is as much an action as a breath is an action. Although we speak in terms of separation, all reality is a part of action. When we divide action in order to discuss it, we in no way change the reality of action, nor alter its nature.

Actions have an electrical reality. Your outer senses do not perceive electrical realities of this nature. Nevertheless, you are a *Gestalt* of electrical actions. Within the physical matter of your chromosomes there are electrically coded systems. These are not the chromosomes themselves. The chromosomes are the physical materialization of the inner electrical data.

Action (you may use the term vitality if you prefer)—action continually attempts to express itself in endless formations. It therefore materializes itself in various forms. I term these forms camouflage. Within your system the camouflage is physical matter. It is impossible for action completely to express itself in any medium.

There is, in no circumstance, any closed system. Action flows within all systems and all realities. Your physical senses are therefore equipped only to perceive the realities within the physical camouflage field.

This does not, however, mean that this is the

only reality. It is simply the only reality that you perceive with the physical senses. In order to perceive other realities you must switch from your outer senses to the inner senses, for the inner senses are clearer, and are equipped to perceive action and reality as they exist independently of the distortions given them by the physical senses.

Because you perceive reality in a limited fashion, this in no way affects the basic nature of reality itself.

The ego attempts to stand apart from action, to view action as the result of ego. However, again, the ego's attempt to stand apart from action in no way changes the nature of action. The ego merely limits its own perception.

There are no limitations to the self, for the self as a part of action has no boundaries except those imaginary ones given to it by the ego. We find, therefore, no limitations to the self, neither top nor bottom. The self is not enclosed within the bony skull. You call your thoughts your own, and yet how do you hold them?

You do not hold them. They are indeed transmitted without your conscious knowledge, and the self expands. Nor is the self limited physically. This idea is the result of your own habit of perception, for chemicals and air and nutrients that you consider not-self enter the self constantly; and that which you consider yourself leaves through the pores of your body.

Nor is the self limited by space and time, for

in dreams you have an actuality that has nothing to do with space nor time, and these dream experiences change and alter your personality, for action must of itself always change. You are familiar only with a small portion of the self. You are more than you know you are, and your journeys range further. . . .

The ego cannot make your heart beat. Why then do you find it difficult to believe that you are more than the ego? For in dreams you meet portions of yourself. You construct realities, and your experience in the dream world is as vivid and valid and as real, in every respect, as your waking experience.

Nor are you fully conscious, in your terms, even in your waking state. You shut out stimuli to concentrate on other stimuli. This is a simplified example of how, in the dream state, you shut out stimuli that is usually accepted by the ego, and become conscious of other realities that you usually ignore in the waking state.

CHAPTER 9

Another Way to Look into the Future
Today: Predictions.

Our Experiments.

Experiments for You.

The seemingly solid table is actually the result of our
own perceptions. To our eyes the table appears solid,
but this does not affect the basic reality of the atoms and
molecules that compose it. It is also possible that past,
present and future are also merely the results of the manner in which we perceive action. Such perception of time
as a series of moments would not affect the basic nature
of time, any more than our perception of the table affects
the actual atoms that form it.

The fact remains that if time does exist in divisions of
past, present and future, then we could never perceive
the future. Many incidences of precognition are documented by the various psychic societies, however. My own
records show that I have seen into the future, and if you
conduct the experiments in this book then you will realize
that precognition is a fact to be accepted, even while it
may not yet be understood.

These considerations make it advisable that we revise
our ideas of what time is, in actuality. In this chapter
we will be concerned with an attempt to put precognition
on some sort of a controlled basis. First, let us consider
the theory of cause and effect, which states that every
effect has a cause that exists before it in time. Again, if

precognition is a reality, then the cause and effect theory must be seriously questioned.

Let's look at an imaginary situation. Mary A, while crossing the street, is hit by a car driven by John F. Imagine also that the accident is seen clairvoyantly by Fred X, two days before it occurs. In space and time as we know it, Mary and John both have to come together at a specific point for this particular incident to happen. Mary's speed in crossing the street and John's speed in the automobile must match so completely that the accident results.

The situation leads to many questions. If Mary did not cross that particular street at that particular time, or if John took another route, would the accident have been prevented? Or would other causes, perhaps psychological ones, have caused a tragedy in any case? Did John have deeply rooted, about-to-explode aggressive tendencies, for example, that would rise up from the subconscious, cause an error of judgment at a crucial moment, and result in an accident? If so, Mary would not necessarily be involved at all.

Or is Mary subconsciously at loose ends, tired of the strain involved in coping with life? Does she subconsciously want to die? Or if she put her trip off until another day, would her mood be changed so that she would step aside from the accident just in the nick of time? On another day would John have his aggressiveness better under control and therefore the vehicle which he drives?

In other words, was the accident predestined to some degree, the result of causes already set up? Or was the accident an event that occurred when two human beings met at a particular point in space and time—the *apparent* result of definite causes, but causes that appear to be causes only after the event?

We simply do not know the answers to these questions. I find it more logical to suppose, however, that the causes seem to be causes only after the event; and that the specific incidents which appeared to cause the accident could have been changed at any point. Now if the accident was seen clairvoyantly by Fred two days earlier,

Fred would simply be tuning into a specific point in space-time. If Fred warned either John or Mary of the tragedy he foresaw, he would be changing the data available to them. If they acted upon this information, it would be possible, at least theoretically, for them to change the apparent effect by refusing to let the apparent causes happen at all.

It is possible that the cause and effect theory is itself a result of our conception of time as a series of moments. This idea is strongly presented in the Seth Material, and excerpts dealing with it will be given at the end of this chapter.

A young acquaintance of ours has been involved in a bizarre series of episodes which seem to suggest that in some cases precognition of an event may allow us to prepare ourselves for the foreseen incident and therefore to affect its nature.

This girl, call her Sarah, tells the following story. As a child she went to an auction with her parents. As they approached the crowd of people, Sarah noticed a particular man, a stranger, who stood nearby. She clutched at her mother and whispered frantically: "That man's going to grab me." Sarah's mother tried to reassure the child, but when Sarah kept repeating the words, she was threatened with a spanking. During the sales when everyone's attention was focused on the auctioneer, the man grabbed Sarah. She screamed, terrified. Her father stopped what seemed to be an abduction, but the man escaped.

Years later when Sarah was a young woman, she sat in a car with her sister. They waited for their mother who was shopping in a nearby store. Not too far away, a man stood by another car. Suddenly Sarah said to her sister, "That man is going to try to get in here." Knowing of the earlier episode and others which will not be related here, her sister said, "Now stop that. Don't start that, it's frightening." Nevertheless, the girls locked the car doors and closed the windows. No sooner had they done so, than the man walked over and tried to force his way into the car. Perhaps because the girls had been forewarned, the man was unsuccessful.

On another, later occasion, Sarah was in a supermarket line, waiting to pay for groceries. A man ahead of her caught her attention. Suddenly she was certain that he was going to bother her. She saw him in her mind try to run her down: in the inner vision he was in an automobile. This seemed so outlandish that she told herself that her imagination was running away with her. Just the same she took her time, waiting until the man had paid for his purchases and left the store.

She watched through the plate glass windows as he got into a car, and drove around the circular drive, out of sight. Then she left. As she reached the center of the parking lot, the other car drove straight at her. As the car approached, she froze, unable to move. The man opened the car door, reached out for her, and shouted, "Get in." She jerked her arm away, yelled for help, and ran back toward the supermarket. This time, the man headed the car at her again. She dodged. He yelled that he'd get her. She reported the incident to the police, although she had been too frightened to get the man's license number.

A few weeks later, however, Sarah saw the same man in the same market. She was with her sister. The two girls went out to the parking lot, found his car, and took down the license number, which they gave to the police department. Police records showed that the man had been a previous offender, in trouble for bothering women. Sarah did not press charges, however, so the man went free.

These incidents are significant from a variety of viewpoints. For one thing, the girl involved is trustworthy. Her parents took her to a psychoanalyst for examination, and there was nothing wrong with her mentally or emotionally. Her history of precognition caused her much embarrassment, and she was bewildered both by the events themselves and her foreknowledge of them. Now she is happily married. Her precognitive abilities still operate.

Now, in the first episode mentioned, as a child Sarah foresaw that a man would grab her. Although she told her parents, the incident happened as she had seen it. In the second episode, however, the precognition caused her to lock the car doors and close the windows. These actions on her part to some extent limited or defined the actions which could then occur. In the last incident it is possible that her foreknowledge acted also as a warning. Undoubtedly it helped her escape what could have been a most unfortunate experience. In this case, also, the fact that she turned the license number in to the police helped confirm the physical reality of the incident.

There is no doubt that Sarah knew what was going to happen. How did she know? Did she telepathically read the men's minds? Did she clairvoyantly see a future event without any telepathy being involved? Is it only coincidence that she was ensnared three times in episodes in which men were the aggressors? Or is it possible that her fear existed first? Perhaps she subconsciously radiated this fear outward, broadcast it so to speak, telepathically, until it was picked up by men who were tempted for their own reasons to respond—men who then broadcast their own answer or intention telepathically before the physical event.

This may be a far-fetched possibility. The episodes themselves are almost unbelievable, however, and yet they occurred. If present theories do not explain human experience, then surely present theories are lacking, and new ones must be found.

We have all had premonitions, hunches, or intuitions that seemed to give us warning of future events, particularly when they involved unpleasant incidents. Science largely discounts such experiences. The various psychic societies, however, are most interested and these societies are staffed by very efficient, well-trained investigators. As far as scientific proof is concerned, such premonitions are difficult to pin down. Usually they do not happen under scientific conditions. Often they occur when we are emotionally upset. We cannot say, "On Friday at 8 P.M. we will have a premonition," and invite the learned gentlemen to investigate. Premonitions do not operate in any such manner.

It is my contention that many hunches and premoni-

are valid instances of extrasensory perceptions. For our own benefit, we can keep careful notes of any premonitions or hunches, making sure that the date and time of day are included. Then if a future event shows that the premonition or hunch was correct, at least we have evidence that we knew about it beforehand. I suggest that you begin keeping such notes. There would be further requirements, however, before such premonitions would be accepted as precognitive by any scientist; and then, with the evidence before him, we could not be certain he would consider it airtight.

Is there any way of making our inner knowledge of future events consistent? Can we train ourselves, put precognition on any kind of a definite basis? Perhaps if we could do so, we would be in a better position to prove our case. At least we would come much closer. Obviously, in most instances, this inner information is not conscious, though a premonition must rise to consciousness or we would never be aware of it.

Usually the ego clamps down rather tightly. My own dreams, recorded carefully now for almost two years, convince me that we do indeed perceive future events. However, some part of the self is able to perceive time as it actually exists. We see into the future as if time were not made up of a series of moments. The only possible answer here is the obvious one: we are able to perceive time in this manner because that is the real nature of time. The apparent series of moments do not really exist.

The experiments in this chapter will let you prove this for yourself—if your dream notes have not already convinced you. You may not perceive events as a whole, you might not even foresee those portions of the events in which you are consciously concerned, but you will find that you, yourself, have important clues today as to what will happen tomorrow.

Impossible? Not at all. First I will outline the experiment for you, and then give you the results of our own. You will need still another notebook. Once a day, whenever it is convenient, sit down alone. You are going to try and predict future events for yourself. Some of your predictions will not be predictions at all. But some will be. If possible, try the experiment at the same time each day. It does not even take five minutes. The subconscious conditioning that is involved is important, however, and you will do better if you set aside the same few moments daily.

Merely write: Predictions for (Monday) made Monday, 8 A.M. or whatever time you set aside. Then write down the number I. Now write down what comes to your mind. Do not consciously try to imagine what you think could happen for the day. You may write one word only, or a phrase, or perhaps a sentence. Do not question what you write. Do not elaborate upon any prediction, or change it. Continue until you have at least five predictions listed for the day.

Treat the whole experiment like a game. Even if the words you write do not seem to make any sense, leave them alone. Do not scratch them out. We are dealing with abilities that are not logical in conscious terms, though you will find that many of your predictions have a logic of their own.

As you have probably guessed, this is only the first part of our experiment. Constantly check what you have written against daily events. If you are seriously following these experiments, you are already checking your dreams and hunches against events in ordinary life. Now check your predictions in the same manner. Check all your notebooks one against the other. Did you predict an event or part of it, and then see another segment of the same event in a dream, for example? Did a telepathic flash, duly written down and dated, reinforce a prediction?

The record-keeping may not seem like your idea of an ESP investigation, but you will find quite an excitement and challenge in records when they are your own. Through such notes you should discover how your own abilities work. Your own records will convince you that extra-sensory perceptions are not esoteric powers but abilities that lie within your own personality.

Obviously we must have adequate methods of judging

the validity of our results. Some predictions will be "better" than others. If, for example, you write that unexpected company will arrive on Monday and then on Monday such unexpected visitors do arrive, your predictions will have more validity if you do not as a rule entertain guests during the week. If your prediction states that the visitors will be two men, and the two men arrive, then the validity of the prediction increases. If, on the other hand, you write down the name John Brown, an old friend you have not seen in years, and John Brown arrives at your house, you can be pretty certain the prediction was a valid one. (Unless, of course, you have received a letter from John Brown that tells you he plans a visit.)

Practice will almost immediately show you what aspects of reality concern you most. Some of you may write down items that deal with world or national events. Others may concern themselves with personal predictions. In all cases, strict records are a necessity. You may also discover that a prediction recorded on Monday may prove out on Wednesday, so give yourself a two- or three-day leeway in this respect.

Now here are some of my own results. In six months, from November 1964 to April 1965, I made 741 predictions. Usually I write five for any given day, though I have slipped up on many weekends and written none at all. Out of these 741 predictions 320 show significant results. These 320 include three grades: what I call direct hits or results that are so close to actual future events that to me no other explanation but precognition is reasonable; results that, while startling, are not on the whole as demonstrable as the direct hits; and results that are still significant but not as clear cut.

As a rule my predictions deal with quite ordinary events, rather than with startling circumstances. Here is a simple example of what I call a direct hit. On March 4 one of my predictions was: stranger to the house. That evening friends visited unexpectedly, bringing with them a complete stranger. The prediction had been written at 8 A.M. I consider this a direct hit for several reasons.

For one thing we live very quietly with a small circle of friends. We do not entertain strangers more than once or twice a year at the very most. In all my other predictions I have only made this same notation twice, and in each instance a stranger did come to our house. No strangers have arrived when they were not predicted.

Here is another example of what is, to me, a good prediction. This incident also points up a tendency for three or more predictions for one day all to apply to the same episode. On January 27 my day's predictions included the following: a secret told . . . a sharp tongue . . . a tease. That same day, late in the afternoon, I was visited by the housekeeper of an elderly neighbor. She told me that she was extremely concerned about my friend and had decided to leave her employ. The friend had "a very sharp tongue" to use her words, and her mind was so warped that she had taken to teasing the housekeeper in disturbing ways, so that the woman was actually very uneasy. She then proceeded, quite against my wishes, to divulge a personal secret that was no one's business but my friend's.

Any one of such similarities between predicted events and actual events could be the result of chance or coincidence. But when 320 out of 741 predictions show varying degrees of significant similarities, then it would certainly seem that this is not a sufficient explanation.

Chance or coincidence seems less and less adequate as a cause when any given future event is seen in part through a prediction, and is also reinforced by precognitive dreams or telepathic flashes.

Consider the following. Earlier I mentioned the dreams in which I received the information concerning the fact that our landlord was thinking of selling the apartment house. The dreams, all occurring within a few evenings, contained the following elements: older people, moving, the possibility that we would look for an apartment. To refresh your memory, read the notations on this dream in Chapter Six. If you recall, these dreams occurred on February 15, 16, and 17.

On February 18 my predictions read: fairly unusual

event . . . a bath . . . a reprimand . . . a splash . . . guest during day. On the 18th, the clairvoyant elements in the dreams proved out. My landlord also showed our apartment to the prospective buyers, a fairly unusual event from my standpoint since in our five years at this address such an incident had never occurred before. But the first words spoken by the real estate woman after she nodded to me were to her customers. "You must see the *bath*room and the shower. It's most unusual. The shower has nine nozzles, the water really comes *splash*ing out." Later, when I spoke to our landlord, who is also a good friend, I *reprimand*ed him, saying that it was foolish to think of selling the house which was good investment property. In this case both my dreams and my predictions gave various aspects of one actual situation of which I could not have otherwise known.

It is true that the predictions were of a trivial nature but such incidents are significant because they bring up strongly the possibility that we know more about the future than we usually suppose. Not only do we seem to know sometimes about distressing or startling circumstances, but mundane matters can also be foreseen. And if those predictions did not apply to those circumstances, then why did I write them down on that day and no other—the one day out of the year when circumstances in the physical world made them significant?

Furthermore, since both the dreams and the predictions seemed to describe various aspects of one actual event, it would appear that coincidence is a poor explanation. If this sort of thing showed up once or twice, we would hardly be justified in drawing any kind of conclusion. But here are some other predictions along with the events that they certainly seem to describe.

Prediction for November 19—a switch of days. On this same date I received first a letter and then a phone call from my in-laws, who twice switched the date for a previously made engagement.

Prediction for November 20—unexpected invitation. On this date a friend dropped in to invite us to dinner.

We had not seen her in months. Just before she knocked at the door, I was strongly thinking about her.

Prediction for December 17—woman in polka dot dress; a study in reactions. On this date a couple we know visited us unexpectedly. The woman wore a polka dot dress. As we sat chatting, our attention was caught by the bizarre behavior of a child in the street. We stood watching at the window for twenty minutes before deciding that the child was either retarded or in need of help. Finally we called the police as the child seemed erratic and incapable of handling himself. This would certainly be a study in reactions.

Prediction for November 16—a stranger to the house. On this evening we went out dancing. The day after I marked the prediction as meaningless. Two days later we discovered that a friend had dropped in on the evening in question with a relative who was a stranger to us.

Prediction for November 10—accident not involving us. That evening a friend told about an accident in which he had been involved a few weeks previously. He had not mentioned it to us earlier.

Predictions for March 5—green light; too many to go; several incidents; someone left behind. On this date I learned that because of several incidents that happened at a previous place of employment, the whole staff was leaving, except one member. I am told that help will be needed and that I will be asked to return to my old position. Here we have too many to go, one left behind, several incidents. I believe that green light refers to my being asked to return. I was being given the green light, symbolically.

Here we have an example of the way in which predictions and telepathic flashes can reinforce each other. My predictions for February 23 read: a lease; a new location; something somewhere else; a happy surprise. The telepathic flash was mentioned earlier. Robert was late for lunch that same day. Suddenly the idea flashed into my mind that he had quit his job, that we would be moving. No sooner did I get the thought than Robert entered with a friend he had met outside. The friend had been on his way here to tell us that they had given notice on their apartment (lease), he had quit his job and was moving to a new location entirely, and looking for a new position. Here we have all the predicted elements, fairly undistorted. From his talk, I took it for granted that he and his wife were leaving immediately and I was then happily surprised to learn that the move would not be made for a month. The distortion in the telepathic communication is apparent. I thought that it applied to Robert, perhaps because I was concerned that he was late.

Here is an example of another instance where predictions and a dream both gave various information concerning an event which later occurred. Predictions for January 29 read: a man we don't know will come here; a message. Predictions for January 30 read: a group of people, 4 or 5; a stiff price; a long haul; something seldom done. On the night of January 29 I had the dream previously mentioned in which I saw myself washing sinks and caring for a patient. The dream had some connection with a hospital also.

On the evening of January 30 the dream checked out when a friend hemorrhaged in rather severe fashion from the nose. This incident was related to the dream. I washed sinks frequently to clean up the blood, and cared for the patient. We called the hospital for instructions and called the young man's parents, asking them to come over (the message). The man's father and his brother (whom we did not know) arrived shortly after, making a group of four. The young man said, and I quote, "What a stiff price to pay for forgetting what the doctor told me." The doctors had warned him against blowing his nose hard as he had had trouble in the past. Certainly the whole evening was fairly unusual (something seldom done), and the long haul could easily refer symbolically to the long night—he slept in our apartment and I kept checking on his condition.

On November 20 one of my predictions read—strange ambiguous letter. On the night of November 23 I dreamed of B. K. My predictions for the following day included

—letter from B. K. On November 24 I received a strange ambiguous letter from B. K., who is not a close friend.

The following example seems to suggest that, between us, Robert and I had fairly full information concerning an event that later occurred. My predictions for February 3 included—a cry; a mistake. My predictions for the next day read—a call; people; unusual incident; something waited for arrives. Robert's predictions for February 3 included the item—after the fall. He repeated this again for predictions on the following day.

On the evening of February 4, an elderly tenant fell in the snowy driveway, breaking her leg. She had mistaken her way to the garbage cans in the dark. Her daughter banged at our door, crying. We called an ambulance for the woman and waited anxiously for it to arrive, as she was in severe pain. People from other apartments and nearby houses gathered about the scene. We arrived, of course, after the fall rather than as the woman actually fell. This became a matter of importance afterwards, when we were questioned for insurance purposes. Here all the elements of my predictions and one of Robert's served to give us a clear picture, but the various circumstances did not make sense until after the event.

Predictions for February 6 and 7 read—turn about; special delivery; reorganize; seven or several; more than is necessary. These seemed to be connected with two separate events. On March 7, the last two predictions—more than is necessary; seven or several—seemed to check out. That evening, entirely unexpected, seven friends dropped in together. The party went on until well after midnight and was rather loud. We thought that there was more drinking and noise than was necessary.

On March 9 the other predictions—turn about; special delivery; reorganize—seemed to check out. On this day the following events happened. I had requested the return of this manuscript from the publishing house as I had heard nothing from them in five months. I was waiting for the manuscript's return. Instead, on March 9, in a complete turnabout, the publishing house asked in a letter that I leave the manuscript with them as they were still considering it. While this was not a special delivery, it was a special delivery to me, as the letter was of some importance. The reason given for the delay was reorganization.

Now you may find that you use a sort of shorthand that is subconsciously significant to you, though at first you may not recognize the connection on a conscious level. Only careful study of your own records can disclose such symbols. Here are some examples from my own records.

Predictions for November 10 included—important letter; 5. On this day I received an important letter from A. K. I could not understand what the number 5 meant and was tempted to cross this off as meaningless until I recalled that years ago A. K. and I had belonged to a group called "The Five."

On six other occasions when the number 5 was written down in the predictions, I received letters from A. K. A. K. worked for a magazine to which I submitted stories and almost without exception the number 5 was written down each time that I heard from him. When he left the magazine, the number 5 was still used, in this case to cover letters from the man with whom I dealt when A. K. was gone.

It is obviously impossible in this book to show more than a sampling from my prediction records. Robert has also carried on his own experiments with predictions, and his results have been as significant as mine. Certain characteristics seem to apply in general. Events are often hinted at rather obliquely; yet, when the foreseen event happens, these elements fit together perfectly like pieces from a jigsaw puzzle. They could not refer to any other event occurring during the time period. Unerringly they appear to point in one direction. This tendency also shows itself in Robert's predictions, and on several occasions between the two of us we will have covered the main aspects of a given event which has not yet occurred.

Symbolism and obliqueness seem to apply to extrasensory experiences in general, yet the data received is far from being vague. The connections are always pertinent, but the significance is not always apparent until after the event happens. The connections are not of the kind you would make on a conscious level necessarily. The type of information that is important to the conscious and subconscious minds seems to differ. The predictions, however, with their results convince me that we do indeed have a knowledge of future events, and that this knowledge can be put on some kind of a consistent basis.

The knowledge can also be used most effectively. In many cases my predictions have prepared me in advance for the events that would follow. This gives a psychological advantage that in my opinion is of great benefit. One day my predictions included a trip. It made no particular sense to me since it was a weekday and we simply never take trips during the week. We had also just returned from our vacation and had no intention of going anywhere else. Later that day we received an urgent call from a member of the family who lives out of town, and we had to make an unexpected journey to the city in which he lived. Since I had spent some time considering the possibilities of a trip as a result of my prediction, I had planned my work so that I could leave, if I needed to. On this account the unaccustomed journey in the middle of the week did not really catch me unawares.

Personal idiosyncrasies will probably show themselves in your records also, as they do in mine. I constantly overestimate good news and underestimate bad news. In many cases, we simply do not want to know what will happen. When Robert was ill with the virus, I could not bring myself to write down predictions at all. This was an understandable but unfortunate and short-sighted reaction on my part. Periods of anxious conscious concern also appear to knock down my average of hits. A week or two may pass in which none of the predictions apply at all. Then there are also periods of high activity in which the predictions constantly prove out almost without fail.

In your own experiments make sure you write down what comes to mind immediately. Do not attempt to elaborate upon what you have written. This could result in the conscious distortion of valid information. More will be said about predictions in the following chapter. Following are some excerpts from the Seth Material that pertain to the nature of time as it is connected with extrasensory perception.

There is much to be explained along many lines which we have only begun to touch upon, for all things are correlated. There is indeed a correlation between our moment points, of which I have spoken, the spacious present, and that portion of the whole self which you call the subconscious.

We are dealing here principally with the essence of action and essentially all apparent divisions are arbitrary, for the sake of explanation. The moment point is in itself arbitrary, an artificial division. The moment point for you is actually composed of the amount of action which you are capable of assimilating within your present framework, for the moment point is indeed a portion of the spacious present.

The subconscious and, in fact, all portions of the self, with the exception of the ego, are capable of assimilating a wider area, so to speak, of action. Therefore, to these other portions of the self, time has an essence different from the one it has for the ego. It can be defined in relationship to many other aspects of reality. In relationship to action and moment points, the ego is indeed that portion of the self that stands at the apex of the moment point, and is limited by the moment point. The ego in this context is the portion of the self which is utterly focused upon, and imprisoned by, the moment point.

The ego is that portion of the self which experiences time as continuity and to whom experience is a series of stimuli and responses carried on one after another. And yet this is in itself a division, so to speak, or a kind of value fulfillment, for the simultaneous nature of a given action is here experienced in a slow motion, as a child must learn to walk before it can run.

The subconscious is not so limited. If you consider the ego at the apex of the moment point and imprisoned within the realm of its own before-and-after, cause-and-effect experience, then you can imagine the subconscious reaching further outward, and seizing upon many other moment points.

It should be easy to see then why the scope of the ego is so sharp and brilliant. Within its limited scope there is intensity of stimulus and response. Indeed, the ego is that part of the self which is plunged into a specific and intense preoccupation with a given field of action or dimension.

The subconscious, reaching outward, reaches also inward. For while there is no real past or present or future within the spacious present, there is indeed an infinity of inward and outward: and again of actions within actions. There is no end to these actions since they are self-generating. The other portions of the inner self reach then even further in all directions, and they therefore envelop many moment points. To many portions of the inner self what you call one moment would correspond to an almost limitless number of moments, for even physical time has no meaning without experience, and without action.

Your whole concept of time is built about your own capacity for perceiving action: as this capacity for perceiving action grows, so indeed do the dimensions of time grow. Conceivably one moment of your time could indeed be also experienced by the whole self as centuries.

This should lead you to understand why physical time is basically meaningless to the subconscious, and why the inner self has at its command a knowledge of past lives and past endeavors. For the inner self, dear friends, these lives are not in the past, nor is the life of the ego necessarily present to the whole self.

For to the whole self, all personalities that compose it exist simultaneously.

It is only the ego that steps from moment to moment, as a man walks from puddle to puddle. It is only the ego who drowns in time. Therefore, since only the ego is momentarily imprisoned within the focus of your field, it is only the ego who probes so slowly into simultaneous action, perceiving it bit by bit, sip by sip. Now you will see what I meant when I spoke of the limitless self, for the whole self is not so bound. The whole self could and does perceive a limitless number of such moment points simultaneously.

CHAPTER 10

More About Predictions.

A Few Seth Predictions.

An Experiment for You.

Here is an experiment for those of you who do not have time to try daily experiments. Take a piece of paper and along the margins write the numbers from 1 to 20. You are going to see how many correct predictions you can make to cover the period of a month. Again, write what comes to mind instantly. If you have trouble getting started, write something down, anything, even if it seems meaningless. Pay as little attention to what you write as possible. Do not be excited if you write a prediction that seems to foretell a joyous event. Do not be downcast if you write a prediction that seems to foretell bad news. Subconscious distortions will probably operate to some extent with everyone, so there is no need to be overly concerned with the meaning of the predictions as you write them. Wait and see. The valid predictions will prove out.

While trying this experiment you may find it advantageous to divert your conscious attention by indulging in some other activity also. Drink a cup of coffee. Watch television if you prefer. Do not try to specify definite dates within the month for your predictions, unless of course, a few dates come to mind spontaneously. Forget your critical faculties when writing down your predictions. Do not make conscious guesses, based upon present knowledge. You will have plenty of use for intellectual criticism and gic when you are ready to evaluate the validity of your results.

In the beginning it is more difficult to establish the validity of a given prediction. Later, your own records will give you hints as to the ways in which you may best handle such data. You will know, for example, how you handle information in general and what symbols you use to express it.

For example, when I began my predictions, I constantly referred to a particular couple as "the turnups," apparently because they would *turn up* at any time, without notice. Many months went by before I realized that there was any connection between this note, turnups, and the couple involved. I also keep record of ordinary physical events, however, and checking my notebooks one day I discovered that whenever the word "turnups" appeared, this couple visited us.

The next time I found myself writing this down as a prediction, I included the note: "I believe that this might refer to Mr. and Mrs. X who always turn up without notice." I never wrote turnups when they did not arrive. Unfortunately the couple moved away so the affair remains in question. Had they remained here for another year or so, I could have checked out this connection more thoroughly. I am reasonably satisfied, however, that the connection was valid. Only a familiarity with your own records can let you discover your own "shorthand."

It is relatively easy to determine the validity of some predictions, when they are clear and concise and the events predicted occur exactly on the day specified. In some cases, however, the prediction may be valid to a greater or lesser extent but you may not be able to check it because the person involved is not available. Or you may discover later that the prediction proved out, after you had discounted it.

If you are doing daily predictions, make sure that you always record the time of day that the predictions are made. One night I wrote a list of predictions at 6:35 P.M. Among them was a notation that C. S. would visit us between 8:30 and 10 P.M. that night. He did not come. The next morning, however, at 9:30 A.M. he did visit us. Laughing, I told him that the time was right enough, but he was supposed to have come the night before. He then asked me what time I had written down the prediction, and I told him. At precisely that time he had been thinking strongly of visiting us, but other business had diverted him. He had looked at the clock to check the time since he had another appointment.

When you write your predictions, probably you will not have any emotional feeling about them at all. Only rarely do I have a conscious feeling that any prediction is right, and when I am consciously certain that one is right, often it does not prove to be valid at all. As a rule you cannot tell by feel but predictions or premonitions that happen spontaneously often are accompanied by a strong emotional content and sense of certainty. Mostly, however, a prediction will seem meaningless, but it will later prove so apt a description of a physical event that I am amazed, later, at my conscious inability to recognize it as valid when writing it down.

If you are seriously trying to develop and use your own abilities, you will not stretch the meaning of any given prediction so that it fits any given event. You will search for any personal shorthand or symbolism that consistently shows itself in your predictions, however, since this is quite legitimate. In some cases these symbolisms must be deciphered, and no one else can do it for you. In my own case, such shorthand does not occur too frequently, but a study of such subconscious language may show us much about the manner in which we inhibit, distort, or express valid clairvoyant information.

After you have become accustomed to experimenting with predictions, the original tendency toward self-conscious concentration will vanish. You will learn to let yourself go, and your predictions will show more consistent results. As with clairvoyant dreams and telepathic flashes, your own predictions may show periodic peaks of activity and inactivity. We cannot always operate at our best it seems, though this is regrettable. If you achieve very good results, and then poor ones, do not be discouraged.

Individuals, regardless of their innate ability, will vary in the degree to which they will allow precognitive material to show itself. Subconsciously, for example, you may at first be afraid of the whole idea of trying to see into the future. If this is the case, it may take a while before you see valid results, or you may simply refuse to allow yourself any success at all in this sort of experiment.

I recommend that all of you who can try the daily predictions. The records are fairly easy to keep. Less than five minutes daily is required to write down the predictions. In many instances you may not write down the exact event that will later occur, even when a prediction is valid. You will, however, if at all successful, write down various aspects of it and aspects that will apply to that event and no other. There is no doubt that time and energy are required to grade your predictions, but the venture is well worth your while.

Suppose that you have at your subconscious command the precognitive knowledge that you will hear from a Miss Y, an acquaintance. Your actual prediction for the day may not be a clear simple statement such as "Miss Y will come here today." Instead of the words Miss Y you may use some shorthand designation that is significant to your subconscious mind. If Miss Y has a disfiguring mole on her cheek, for example, you may write, "Miss Mole" or "mole on check," in which case you might never realize that the prediction was a valid one, because you did not know how to interpret the language used by your own subconscious.

Robert's predictions one day included the word, all by itself, "halitosis." It meant nothing to him. That day he received a letter from a doctor, the only man we know who has a severe case of halitosis. We had often talked about the man's condition, between ourselves. Robert's predictions had never included the word halitosis before, nor had we ever received a letter from the doctor before.

We cannot expect, much less demand, that the intuitive part of the self operate in the manner used by the conscious logical mind. On the other hand, in its own way the intuitive self uses symbols that are just as crisp and apt. They simply may not be the ones that we are familiar with on a conscious basis.

The daily prediction experiment is an excellent method of training yourself to use your own abilities—and it is great fun besides. The time element in connection with predictions is an interesting study in itself. A note concerning a future event made on Monday morning for Tuesday may prove valid on Monday afternoon, for example. You may take time leaps ahead, also, that you do not anticipate. All of this serves to acquaint you with the ways in which *you* work, even though it does sometimes add to the difficulty of grading your results.

Here is a case that brings up the question of a time leap. For November 24 my predictions included the following—A. F. will visit; an amazing coincidence. A. F. not only did not visit that day but we did not see him until December 10. I had long ago marked the predictions off as meaningless.

During A. F.'s next visit on December 10, however, I happened to mention that a friend knew of a monk who had heard about the Seth sessions and was highly interested in them. The monk resided at a nearby monastery. "Do you mean Father X?" A. F. said, surprised. I answered, "Yes, I do. How did you know?" It developed that A. F. had received a letter from this same monk in connection with a business matter. A. F. does not even know the friend who told me of the monk's interest, and A. F. does not live in the same city with the monk, my friend, or myself.

I considered this quite a coincidence. It is even more startling when you consider that both A. F.'s visit and mention of an amazing coincidence were listed as predictions for the same day and that the notes were written a month earlier.

I did not change my records, however, listing this as a valid prediction, because of the time lapse involved, but I did go back and make a note of the circumstances. It is very possible that important clues as to how clairvoyance works may be hidden in such instances, however, and I suggest that you watch your own records carefully so that evocative happenings such as this one do not escape your notice. As such circumstances collect in written records, we may be able to find patterns that will open up areas of knowledge.

If you write down a prediction concerning a particular person and the prediction does not seem to prove out, check with the person involved if possible. On several occasions I wrote that specific persons would visit on a definite day and they did not. At least twice it turned out that the persons had been seriously considering such a visit at the time that I made the predictions. Circumstances just happened to be right, so that they remembered the time accurately. Other predictions may be valid but circumstances may prevent us from questioning the individuals. We cannot expect 100 per cent accuracy in any case. Certainly you should not take it for granted that the majority of predictions are accurate though they do not prove out. You should, however, keep it in mind that some may be valid even though their validity cannot be proven.

The Seth Material contains some predictions, although we have not tried to force the sessions into any mold. We have not tried to get Seth to make predictions. To date, Seth has made no predictions which have not worked out. In some, a time element of three years or so is involved, and of course we will not know about these until the time has passed. Seth's idea of time is certainly different from ours, however. When he says that a given event will happen soon, then I take this to mean within a week or so. To Seth "soon" can take six months. Some of the Seth predictions involved personal events in the lives of friends or acquaintances and these will not be discussed here, except for a few. These few, however, will serve to give the reader an idea of the nature of the predictions in general.

On March 9, 1964, Robert asked Seth about the condition of a sick friend who was in the hospital. Seth gave the date April 15 as being a significant one for her, but added no other details. Our 44th Seth session fell on April 15. Robert asked the following question: "Can you tell us anything about Mrs. Y tonight?"

Here is the answer as given:

Only that today, April 15, or rather late this evening, actually 2 A.M. your time, she will undergo a severe crisis, and that rapid deterioration of brain tissue will develop. She is over, or will be over, the worst hump by then.

A few days later I called the hospital and learned that Mrs. Y had been discharged. I took this to mean that despite Seth's remarks, her condition had improved. On April 22, however, some relatives of Mrs. Y's stopped in to visit us. They told us that on April 15, Mrs. Y upset the entire hospital floor, and the hospital officials insisted that she be removed to a sanitarium. Her condition had deteriorated to such a degree that she displayed the following symptoms of mental disorder: yelling, throwing things, screaming, running down the hospital halls, calling for help from the police.

During the 68th session, our friend Bill Macdonell was a guest. Bill was planning a vacation at Provincetown, and Robert asked Seth if he could tell us anything about Bill's vacation in advance. This was the answer received:

He will, of course, go to the seashore. There is a man, perhaps fifty years old, with prickly hair, with whom he will become acquainted. I see a rowboat with a symbol of some sort on it.

In the 75th session, July 24, 1964, while Bill actually was in Provincetown, Seth offered us the following information though we had not questioned him:

Your friend has made two friends, one older and one approximately his own age. He is, of course, near water. He has been at a bar with a large keg in it. There are two houses nearby, and a front room across from a beach. There is a boat and a dock. I also believe he was in a group with four men. Maybe something to do with a string of shells also.

There had been no correspondence between Bill and ourselves. On his return, August 29, he visited us. He was not positive of the exact date but on or about July 29 he was at a party with two acquaintances he had made during vacation. One was a man in his fifties, with a prickly brush cut, and another was a man two years younger than himself. (Bill is in his middle twenties.) Two other men were also present at the party.

Thus he was in a group with four men. The party itself was held in a cottage that was connected with another cottage (two houses), in a front room that overlooked the beach. According to Bill it is unusual in Provincetown to find a front room that has a view on the water, since in most cases the cottages are arranged in helter-skelter groupings, with the back, rather than front, rooms facing the beach. There were many boats tied to a dock outside.

Immediately after the party Bill and his friends went to a bar which was distinguished from others by its unique decoration—one huge keg, cut in half, each half set into the wall. Other bars were decorated with small kegs, but this large one was very striking. The bar and the cottages were about three blocks apart. (According to Seth, they were nearby.)

Bill did not know what the string of shells referred to, except that shell ashtrays were used at the party. He did not recall a boat with symbols on it. Later Seth said that the boat was green and Bill did remember a green boat tied across from the cottage, since he made a painting of it. He also made a painting of the general area, including the cottages.

Seth also predicted the sale of this manuscript by name, on September 28, 1964. On November 4, he said that a sale had developed, and that future sales having to do with short stories would also result.

They have not actually developed, but the framework that will assure them has already been laid. A woman might have something to do with one sale through influence.

On May 5, 1965, the book contract was signed, partly through the influence of a woman editor, though in the past I had been dealing with Mr. Fell and did not know that the previous editor had left the firm to be replaced by a woman. On May 25, shortly after the book contract was signed, I sold a short story to a national magazine. Thus in May, the book sold as Seth predicted, a woman was involved in its sale, and a short story was also sold.

None of these is a spectacular prediction. Seth did pinpoint the very day of Mrs. Y's crisis, but the predictions concerning the book took almost half a year to prove out. Recently Seth mentioned a particular stock and predicted that it would begin to fall steadily downward. Since the prediction it has fallen five points. He also gave us some general information concerning our attendance at the Hypnosis Symposium at State University College, Oswego, N.Y., in July, 1965. Events developed there as he said that they would.

As far as your own experiments are concerned, watch out for the following: predictions that all apply to one event; subconscious designations (such as the Miss Mole example) which you may consistently use to name certain individuals. These are subconscious shorthand symbols. Make certain that you always record the time that your predictions were made and the day for which you

are trying to predict. Give yourself two or three days'
leeway before grading your results.

There is also a possibility that on occasion some predictions may apply to not one but two definite events.
Our own records seem to point out this tendency. I will
mention the following example from our own records.

These particular predictions are interesting from two
viewpoints. First, they demonstrate how Robert and I
appear to collaborate to pinpoint a future event. Second-
ly, they illustrate single predictions that apply to two
separate situations. If this last possibility turns out to be
a valid characteristic of some precognitive material, then
subconscious shorthand, at times so crisp and concise,
is also so accurate that it fits two events at once yet is not
applicable to any other events.

For June 30 my predictions included the following:
several questions, several times; tell me again; the journey, a long way; begin this over. Robert's predictions
included the notation: the investigator.

We had not seen each other's predictions. On the day
projected, an insurance investigator knocked at our door.
He asked me questions about a neighbor who had moved
away. He did not at first tell me the reasons for his questions, and I refused to answer them. Finally he told me
his business and I let him in, asking him to repeat his
questions. The neighbor involved had moved to California. Here all the predicted elements appeared in the
actual event. The investigator, one of Robert's predictions, could not have been more specific.

The same predictions also seemed to fit perfectly
another situation which happened the same day. We had
told our landlord that friends of ours wanted to rent a
vacant apartment downstairs. They had not as yet given
any down payment on the rent, and in the meantime a
woman called who also wanted the apartment. We felt
rather responsible for the situation and I went to a corner
phone booth to call our friends. They were not home. I
was given another number to call. For a half hour I was
involved in asking several questions several times as

we tried to get the story straight. I did indeed feel like an investigator. Three of the predictions: several questions, several times; tell me again; and the investigator also seemed to apply here.

I realize that these are not spectacular incidents. We are concerned with studying the ways in which the subconscious handles material which is not known to the conscious mind, however, and any characteristics that seem to show themselves in predictions should be carefully scrutinized. Both the visit of the insurance investigator and the scrambled telephone calls helped distinguish that particular day from other days, and both situations seemed to be at least partially foreseen.

Daily predictions will give us sufficient data with which to work. Little information can really be received through the mere recording of more unusual spontaneous precognitions. As daily records accumulate we will have more and more data which can then be examined in the hopes that it will divulge the nature and characteristics of precognitive material.

Because all investigation of clairvoyance must necessarily involve our concept of time, the following Seth excerpts are included here. In them, Seth discusses time in relation to electric impulses and presents a simple analogy.

Excerpts from Session 54

The old analogy, rather trite I'm afraid, is still a good one. Walking through a forest you find many trees. Time can be conceived of as the entire forest. You, however, see a tree in front of you and call it the future. You think that the tree was not there before because you had not come to it yet. The tree behind you, you call the past. You are walking, so to speak, along one narrow

path, but there are many paths. The forest exists
as a whole. You can walk forward and backward,
though you are only now learning how.

We will carry this analogy further. We will call
this whole forest the spacious present. The trees
are compared to consciousness, all existing simultaneously; and yet this forest of the spacious present does not take up space as you think of space.

There is no past, present or future in your terms
within it, but only a now. Because of the endless
possibilities within this now, durability is maintained in terms of value fulfillment, the fulfillment
of literally endless values. Therefore, the forest is
constantly expanding. It is not expanding in terms
of space or time, but in terms of fulfillment of
abilities and values that may be constructed upon
various levels and in various guises, your present
field of existence being one.

Excerpts from Session 125

You conceive of action in terms of time, since
within your physical world a given action appears
to take up time, almost in the same way that a
chair seems to take up space. The chair, of course,
does not take up space, but is part of what you
call space. Nor does the action take up time. It is
part of what you call time. . . .

It is difficult to explain this to you, since old
concepts must be used in a new way. But . . . we
have been speaking of the electrical reality of

thoughts and emotions, and of dreams, and of all such experiences which appear to be purely psychological in origin, and which take up no space in your physical universe.

I have also mentioned that the electrical field has its own variety of dimensions, with which you are not familiar. Depths are contained within this system that are not depths in terms of space, but rather depths and dimensions in terms of varying intensities. There is also here a duration that is closely connected with intensity, but not with continuity in terms of time.

In this electrical system, a travel through time would merely involve a travel through intensities. There is constant motion in this system, as in all others, and the constant motion makes motion possible within your own system: and time is indeed an electrical impulse that grows by intensity, and not by moments.

To speak of backward and forward is meaningless. There are only various electric pulsations of varying intensities; since strong intensities are natural results of weaker intensities, it would be meaningless to call one present and one past. Yet within your physical field, and with physical time, you ride the waves of these pulsations, so to speak.

When the pulsation is weak, you call it past. When it is strongest, you name it the present, and one that seems to you not yet as strong as present, you name future. For you make the divisions yourselves. In such a manner you have made the framework and all the possibilities, potentials and limitations inherent within a system set up with a divided time field.

CHAPTER 11

Have You Lived Before?

Experiments for You.

Our Experiments.

Reincarnation, Fact or Fiction?

Is it possible that we have lived before? Many millions of human beings believe that we are born time and time again, that our human potentialities can never be fully developed in the brief span of one lifetime, but that they grow and mature through succeeding reincarnations. Suppose for a moment that this is true. Our next question would be: If we have lived before, then why don't we remember our own past lives on a conscious basis?

First, let me ask you another question. You know for a fact that you were an infant and a child before you were an adult, yet how much of your own childhood do you remember consciously? Very little. The bulk of such memories are now part of the subconscious mind. If we cannot remember experiences that belong to this existence, it should not be surprising if memories of past lives are also repressed.

Forgotten events from childhood can be recalled through hypnosis. If reincarnation is fact and not fiction, we should be able to recall past lives through hypnosis also. Even in this case we would not know if such memories were valid until we received enough solid information to check against existing historical records and public documents.

As far as absolute proof is concerned, consider the

difficulty involved in proving a simple fact that is not immediately demonstrable. Suppose you wish to prove that the boy who sat behind you in fifth grade wore a brown suit on May 6, 1938. Imagine that this fact stayed fresh in your mind through all these years, though other memories vanished from your consciousness. You may know beyond doubt that the boy's suit was brown, but proving it would be most difficult.

For one thing, records would not exist as to the color of the clothing worn by any of your classmates on any given day. Even if you tracked down the individual involved and questioned him, you would be no closer to proof. Now a man, the individual would have no idea as to what sort of clothing he wore. If a black and white photograph had been taken, the question of the color of the boy's suit would still not be settled. Only a color photograph would suffice as evidence, and then it would be necessary to prove without doubt that the photograph had been taken on the day in question.

If reincarnation is a fact, then the problems of collecting evidence will be overwhelming. Even if we take it for granted that the information received through hypnosis and other methods is correct, we would have to become involved in an effort to check this data through records, private letters, old newspapers, and numberless other sources. Even if we could prove beyond doubt that John X somehow had an intimate knowledge of the seventeenth century life of a particular bishop, for example, this would not necessarily be evidence that John X had once lived as that bishop. He could have collected such information subconsciously in some manner. He could somehow be in communication with the spirit of that bishop. Granted, these explanations would be as amazing as the reincarnation thesis; nevertheless if such detailed knowledge of the past was proven beyond doubt, they would then have to be considered.

There are already cases on record where living persons insist that they have lived other lives, displayed intimate knowledge of the dead individuals involved, were confronted by the living relatives of the dead person, and correctly identified the relatives although they have been introduced as strangers.

Two such cases appeared in India in this century. It may be a coincidence that these were discovered in a country in which reincarnation is accepted. Or it may be that such incidents are not ridiculed in India, and therefore more apt to come to light. In these particular cases, memories that appeared to be valid previous life memories were not buried in the subconscious, but were at a conscious level.

Even if reincarnation is a fact, however, as a rule the ego would not be aware of it. Theoretically, any previous life recollections could be brought to the surface by a method which would relax the conscious ego sufficiently so that the inner data could make itself known. Hypnotism should prove the most effective method of uncovering such information. Automatic writing may be another. Simple word association could be useful. There are also cases on record in which memories that seemed to be of previous life origin were uncovered during psychoanalytic sessions.

It is true that most scientific investigations into ESP are not concerned with reincarnation. Since the subject is often implied in any study of mediums, however, it is of great interest in connection with psychic phenomena, and therefore is a legitimate area of discussion in this book. Automatic writings, automatic speech and spirit controls often claim to originate with reincarnated personalities. This does not necessarily mean that reincarnated personalities are, in fact, involved. But any investigation must at least take the possibility into consideration.

No one can tell you if you have lived before. If a large percentage of the human race alive today has also lived in the past, then the evidence rests within each individual, in those areas of the personality beneath the ego. The only answer lies in self-investigation. Complicated technological paraphernalia will not help us explore the realities of the human personality. Whatever answers may be possible will be found only through exploration of the inner self.

This chapter will include instructions for an experiment that will allow you to achieve the freedom necessary to search for the existence in yourself of any previous life memories. I am including here excerpts from a transcript of a hypnosis session with Robert as subject and myself as hypnotist. This represents our first attempt to regress a personality beyond birth. The subject was put into a deep trance state through induced relaxation, and the following suggestion was then given: "As odd as this sounds, when I count to eight you will see scenes from a time before you were Robert Butts." This was repeated several times and the count from one to eight was given.

QUESTIONS	REPLIES
What do you see?	Puddle.
What is your name?	Josie.
How old are you?	I'm five.
What are you doing?	Playing around a horse.
Whose horse?	Some man's.
Where do you live?	In a city.
What city?	Maryland.
Do you live in a house?	Yes . . . steep.
What is your last name?	Williams.
Do you have brothers and sisters?	Five.
What does your daddy do?	He shoes horses.
Do you know the name of the city in Maryland, or is Maryland the name of the city?	No.
What is the name of the city in which you live?	Maryland.

"When I count to eight, you will be ten years old." This suggestion was given several times, and the count was then given.

What is your name?	Joe.
Joe or Josie?	Joe. (Answers impatiently.)
Are you a boy or girl?	I'm a boy. (Subject sounds disgusted.)
Where do you live?	I'm in a stable.
In a stable?	Yes, Horseshoes . . . There's hammering on the shoes.
Do you have brothers and sisters?	Four.

(Previously the answer five was given to this question.)

Whose stable is it?	My father's. (Here again the subject sounded disgusted at my lack of knowledge.)
Tell me about it.	Sparks on the hot shoes. . . . The sledge hammer rings. Sparks and flies. The door is open.
What is the street?	The smell of horses, straw. . . .
What kind of street is it?	Oh. It's a stone street.
What is the name of the town?	Maryland.
What is the name of the street?	Spencer Street.
Do you live there?	Next door. Upstairs.

This hypnosis session was held initially to relieve the subject of annoying back symptoms. In this it was successful not only in minimizing the pain involved, but in helping the subject to understand many of the inner reasons that brought about the condition. We had not planned to attempt any regression experiences of the kind described. When I discovered that the subject was in an excellent trance state, however, I decided to turn the session into those channels, after first checking with the subject.

Because this was our first experience, it suffers from

several flaws. For one thing, the subject was not given sufficient time to answer the questions. He saw and felt much more than I gave him the opportunity to describe. Many questions should have been followed up, but the session lasted an hour and a half as it was, and I did not want to prolong it.

Many obvious questions were neglected for this reason, such as the all-important matter of the year of Joe's birth, and the country in which Maryland was a city. At the time I took it for granted that Maryland was the state, and that the subject was confused. Actually such a supposition has no place in this kind of session. Also it may be advantageous to count backward rather than forward, as the backward count would be more suggestive of going back in time.

The experience was very vivid for the subject. The sensual data was fresh and immediate. The tone of his voice was a convincing portrayal of a child's. He became quite impatient with me several times. I had taken it for granted that Josie, the name given at the age of five, was a female name. Later, when the subject used the name Joe he was very cross with me for asking if he was a male or female.

This session showed us that these experiences of the subject's were as vivid as those in more ordinary age regression. If you recall, it was mentioned earlier that in ordinary age regression the actual early events are relived, rather than simply recalled. And in this session, Robert felt that the events were happening in fact. The session was recorded. We had just purchased our recorder, however, and I was not too familiar with its operation. The subject's voice is fairly clear; unfortunately the traffic outside is fairly clear also.

Before we go on to your own experiment, it may be interesting here to see what Seth had to say about Robert's hypnosis session. Here we find the Seth Material adding to the data received through hypnosis as Seth adds details to the life supposedly lived by Robert in the Joe Williams existence. The following is a brief excerpt from Seth session 59.

Steep steps led to your house at that time. Your wife's name, I believe, when you grew, was Nell Brownell. Your name was Williams. You met Ruburt in Boston, in this country, after an absence from him. You did have five children in the family, that is, you had two brothers and three sisters, one sister dying before you were grown.

Maryland was not in this country. You came here, to Boston. Maryland is a city. It is not a state in your country . . . records may possibly be found in Boston. Your mother's name at that time was Josephine. You were then slim and disciplined to some degree, ending up with four children and a wife who became an invalid. Your occupation was that of an episcopal clergyman.

There was a church of brick, in a neighborhood at first pleasant and then deteriorating. An old mansion across the street was turned into a grocery store. There was, later, a dress shop nearby, and from the third story window, front, you could see the water. You were ordained under peculiar circumstances, not being educated in orthodox terms. When you migrated to Boston you took the name of Drake. I do not know the first name. You were young when you migrated and the ship was three days late.

Smallpox broke out in the hold. A captain took you under his wing. You did not sign on as you should and you were discovered, but you reminded him of a nephew, last name Phillips, and he protected you. . . . You also had one illegitimate child.

Please understand that we are not claiming that the Joe Williams existence happened in fact. We are claiming that it is *possible* that through hypnosis Robert did actually reach memories of a past life in which he was Joe Williams. We do know that this experience was as vivid to him as more ordinary age regression experiences through hypnosis, and psychologists are quite willing to accept age regression. Their own experiments show, for example, that when the subject says he is five years old he then performs on psychological tests as a five-year-old. Until we accumulate much more information on the Joe Williams existence, all we have is some highly evocative material. Our own time is also limited and reincarnation is only one of the subjects in which we are interested.

The following experiment will allow you to explore the usually inaccessible areas of your own personality for the existence of any possible previous life memories. I do not suggest that you hypnotize anyone else, or allow yourself to be hypnotized unless you obtain a good background knowledge of hypnosis through reading and study. This experiment will involve self-hypnosis.

Again, if reincarnation is a fact, it is very possible that hypnosis can lead us to recover some of these lost memories, in the same way that it can allow us to recover forgotten incidents from childhood. However, unless we are willing to accept such information on faith, we cannot just take it for granted that the material is valid. We must make every attempt to check it against existing records and documents.

In order to check the validity of such data, it is obvious that first the information must be collected—and from the subconscious personality, since the conscious mind is aware of only a fraction of our past experience at any given time. Hypnosis is the best method of reaching the subconscious that we know.

To begin the experiment, then, put yourself in a trance state, following the instructions given earlier in this book. Before the session begins, however, write down suggestions for use after self-induction. After you have put yourself into a trance state, these suggestions can then be read to you by someone else. If you own a tape recorder, you can dispense with the other person if you desire, pretape the suggestions and then play them back. For that matter, you can pretape a self-induction, following earlier instructions, and tape the whole session. You can then hear your own voice later, with the changing inflections that you may use. You will respond to the taped voice as you would to any voice, regardless of the source.

During the first few sessions, deal with simple age regression in this life alone. This will build up your own confidence, and is a fascinating experience. You will be astonished at the extent of your own subconscious memories. Many of these can be checked with your own relatives.

After putting yourself in the trance state, either have another person give you the following suggestions, or play the pretaped suggestions on your recorder. "I am going to count backwards from ten to zero. When the count is completed you (I) will be fifteen years old." Repeat the suggestion several times. Count slowly backward (or have the other person do it.) Suggest that only pleasant episodes will be remembered. At the end of the count, the following questions can then be asked. Again, these can be prepared, or given by another person.

How old are you?

Where are you?

Who is with you?

What year is it?

The questioning will be far easier and more flexible if questions are asked by another person. Prerecorded questions cannot take your answers into account. Questions should follow naturally from the answers that are given. Therefore, if you find yourself in a classroom at age fifteen, the person who is asking the questions can use this as a springboard to ask you the name of the teacher and to request that you identify some of your classmates.

Unless the session is being recorded, you need someone with you in any case to take notes. Above all, do not rush. Make sure that you have all the time you want to answer each question before going on to the next.

When the episode at fifteen seems completed, then the above procedure should be repeated, and suggestions given that on repeat of the count, you will be five years old. Again, suggest that only pleasant episodes will be remembered. The whole procedure may then be followed through, this time regressing you to the age of one year. I suggest that you take two or three separate sessions for the experiment thus far.

Obviously, questions should be varied, according to the age to which you have regressed. I will include an excerpt from one of our age regression sessions, and you will quickly see the sort of questions that are appropriate. Unless you carry on intensive investigations over a period of years, do not specifically suggest that possible previous birth or death experiences be recalled.

It should be mentioned again that events in age regression will not be remembered but actually relived, with all the sensual data that was present in the original experience.

The following is part of an age regression session, again with Robert as subject and myself as hypnotist. You can also use the format for your own experiments. You can, of course, return to any age. The designations fifteen, five and one are merely suggestions on my part. Any years can be chosen.

Here the trance has already been induced and the first count given.

QUESTIONS	REPLIES
How old are you?	Three.
What day is it?	Tuesday.
Where are you?	In my room.
What do you see?	The floor and window.
What else?	Tree, street outside window.
Where is your mother?	She must be downstairs.
Do you have any brothers?	One. (Robert has two

brothers but the youngest was not born when he was three years old.)

Are you happy? — I don't know. I'm alone.

Now you will let the scene fade. You will let the scene fade. I will count backwards again from ten to zero. At the end of the count you will be two years old. (Suggestion was repeated several times, and the count given.)

How old are you?	I'm two.
Where are you?	On the grass.
Is it summer?	Yes. Nice day. I crawl under the bench . . . with the feet . . . black pants. They're sitting over me.
Who?	I don't know. I think I hear my mother.
In a backyard?	Yes.
What do you call your mother?	Mot—her. (Long, drawn-out sounds.)
What do you call your father?	Da—ddy. (Same long, drawn-out sounds.) I thought I saw a dog. Brown.

I then removed the scene from his mind, suggested that at the next giving of the count he would be one year old. Then the count was given.

How old are you?	I'm one.
Where are you?	Bathroom.
What are you doing?	In . . . water.
In a tub?	No. Something like it. On stilts.
Is someone washing you?	Yes. My mother.
What do you call her?	Ma Ma. (This was uttered very much like a cry, quite different from the "Mother" given at the age of 2.)

| Can you see the room? | Pictures on the wall . . . paper. |
| What does your mother look like? | Brown hair. Small front tooth. (The subject's mother has had white hair as long as he can remember, consciously. It was still brown, however, when he was an infant.) |

Again, the subject felt that he was not given sufficient time to describe what he saw and felt at the time. For example, he actually felt his mother's arms around him. The immediacy of such experiences is obviously quite different from the secondhand feelings connected with incidents that are consciously recalled.

The age regression sessions are only a part of this experiment, however. When you have practiced with age regression, and are familiar with the sensations involved, then proceed with your attempts to uncover subconscious memories of a possible previous life.

After self-induction, have another person give you the usual age regression suggestions. This time, however, go from the present to a very early age, say, one year or six months. Have a brief question and answer period, then have the other person give you the following suggestions:

"I am going to count backwards from ten to zero. Now as odd as this might seem, when the count is finished you will see scenes from a time before you were (give present name)." Repeat the suggestions, give the count, and then proceed.

Here are some initial general questions that can be asked.

What do you see?
Where are you?
How old are you?
In what country are you?
What is the year?
What is your name?

I have purposely placed the question of identity at the end of the list. This enables you to get your bearings before dealing with another identity, and makes the transition easier. If you maintain that you are an adult, then the following questions may be asked.

Are you married?

What is your (husband's or wife's) name?

Do you belong to any organizations? Which ones?

Who is the president, king or ruler of your country?

What is your occupation?

What are your parents' names?

From what country did your parents come?

Do you read a daily newspaper? Which one?

You cannot rush this experiment. Take time to get full answers. If you maintain that you are a child, then obviously the above questions cannot be asked. Questions suitable to the age should be substituted. A child, for example, may or may not know the kind of government under which he lives. If further information is desired, suggestions may be given so that with the regular counting procedure, the age of the personality will be advanced to adulthood.

The person who helps you in this experiment must be someone you can trust. Husband and wife teams should work well, if the relationship is a good one. Along with your self-induction, always include the suggestion that you will come out of the trance whenever you choose, at the count of three or at a specified time. This puts the control in your own hands, and on any sense of uneasiness, you may end the trance. Always make sure, however, that you are returned to your present identity and the present age. This is done as follows. Instruct the person with whom you are working to give these suggestions if you seem at all tense:

"Now I am going to count from one to ten. When the count is completed you will be back in the present time. You will be [insert present name] at age [insert present age]." The suggestions should be repeated, and then the count should be given. There is very little possibility that you would refuse to make the transition to your present personality. Such a situation is so improbable that it need not concern us. Nevertheless, no session of this kind should be ended without including the suggestions given above. When the count has been given, you should then be asked your name and age and the session should not be ended until you correctly give your present age and identity. This procedure should also be followed to end an ordinary age-regression session. It is a good idea to insert in your trance induction the suggestion that you will be refreshed and relaxed at the end of the session.

Careful records should be kept at all times. When the work of collecting information in this manner results in an accumulation of data, then it is important that it be checked against public records, old courthouse files, etc. This is obviously a difficult and time-consuming procedure, but we cannot just take it for granted that our information is correct. If names and dates and locations do check out against historical documents, then we will be closer to some kind of scientific proof.

It must be restated here that while we can get through hypnosis material that seems to be of previous life origin, we must then try to discover if this information is what it appears to be, or if it is merely subconscious playacting. The psychologists themselves do not know enough about either the mind or hypnosis to say categorically that such apparent memories are subconscious fabrication; but I doubt if you would find any who would say that they are from previous lives either.

Now while hypnotism is an excellent method of trying to uncover such material, automatic writing or automatic speech are other methods. We have discussed automatic writing earlier in this book. When using it for this purpose, simply suggest at the start that your subconscious will use your hand to express itself on this subject. If you have already had some success with automatic writing since beginning this book, it is possible that this method will prove effective for you. Use the procedure given previously.

Those of you who have experimented with automatic speech may find yourselves giving material concerning reincarnation, as I have done. If so, check your material against itself. Ask the same questions several times, or have someone else ask them, and see if you get the same answers. Make up a list of questions and have them read aloud to you when you are delivering a session.

Any such data received through the "Ouija" board should also be studied.

This chapter has been mainly concerned with hypnosis in its relation to uncovering any possible previous life memories. But if reincarnation is a fact of life, one that we have long denied, clues to its existence will also be found in other aspects of our normal lives. Indications may appear in our dreams. Past lives may even affect our present health. In the next chapter we will discuss reincarnation in relation to dreams, personality tendencies and patterns of health and illness.

The following excerpts from the Seth Material present a logical framework within which reincarnation could operate.

Excerpts from Session 126

Even the electrical reality of a dream is decoded, so that its effects are experienced not only by the brain, but in the furthest reaches of the most minute cells of the human body. Dream experiences, long forgotten, are forever contained as electrically coded data. If an effect is felt in any one portion of human experience, then you can be sure that it is felt in all other possible ways, whether or not such an effect is immediately obvious.

Every effect of any kind, experienced by the human being, exists as a series of electrical signals and codes that in themselves form a pattern that is an electrical pattern.

They exist within the cells, or I should more properly say that the cells form about them. These electric coded signals then form electric counterparts of complete experience, as it has been felt by a given individual. The pattern is independent of the physical system, while residing in it. Each individual from birth on forms his own counterpart from built up, individual, continuous electric signals. At physical death his personality then exists in more or less complete form, and of course escapes the sort of ending that it would suffer if it were an integral part of the physical system.

The electrical pattern *is* the personality, with all the experiences of earthly time. It can then join or partake of the inner self. Though the ego was adapted originally by the inner self and was also a product of physical heredity and environment, it does not die, but its existence is changed from physical reality into electrical reality. It is still individual. No individuality is lost but becomes part of the inner self, and its experiences are added to the total experiences of the many personalities that have composed the inner self.

Excerpts from Session 132

I have mentioned that the electrical universe is composed of electricity that is far different from your idea of it. Electricity as you perceive it within the physical system is merely like an echo emanation, or a sort of shadow image of these infinite varieties of pulsations. These pulsations give reality and actuality to many phenomena with which you are familiar, but which do not appear as tangible objects within your physical system.

We have seen that all experience is retained in electrically coded data within the cells, and that the material of the cells forms about this coded experience. The ego begins, sparked into being by the inner self, greatly influenced by heredity and environment. . . . This ego as it continues to exist gradually builds up an electrical reality of its own as its experiences form into coded data within the cells.

At any given point the ego is complete within electrical reality, as it is psychologically complete within the physical system. This includes, of course, the retention of its dreams as well as the retention of purely physical data.

The electrical system possesses many dimensions of reality that cannot be perceived within the physical system. So far your scientists have only been able to study electricity by observing their projections of it that are perceivable within their frames of reference. As their physical instruments become more sophisticated, they will be able to glimpse more of this reality. But since they will not be able to explain it within their known system of references, many curious and distorted explanations of reported phenomena will be given.

It is most difficult at this time to hint at the myriad complexity and dimension of the electrical actuality as it exists, when you consider that each of your own thoughts is composed of a unique intensity of impulse, shared by nothing else, and that this same may be said for every dream that you will have in your lifetime; and that all this experience is gathered together in particular ranges of intensities, again completely unique, codified; and this, the summation of all that you are, exists in one minute range or band of intensities. Then you will see how difficult it is to explain.

All human beings are also in the same manner electrically composed and everything else, with few exceptions, within the physical field whether or not it exists within physical matter. Your physical field is contained within its own unique range of intensities, a tiny band of electrical impulses a million times smaller than any one note picked out at random from the entire mass of musical composition that has been written or ever will be written. Yet as you know this is not meant to give you a sense of futility, for uniqueness brings its own responsibility.

All motion is mental psychological motion, and all mental and psychological motion has electrical reality. The inner self moves by changing or moving through intensities from your physical field. Each new psychological experience opens up a new pulsation intensity, and gives greater actuality within the electrical system. To move through intensities within the electrical system gives the result of moving through time within the physical system.

CHAPTER 12

Reincarnation, Family Relationships, and the Personality.

Do You Remember Past Lives in Your Dreams?

A General Discussion.

If reincarnation does exist, then there must be some sort of retention of knowledge and identity to connect one existence to another. Otherwise, at least to me, the whole theory would be meaningless. This continuity of self would not necessarily have to be conscious, but in one way or another it would have to be a part of our individuality.

The excerpt at the end of the last chapter should have given you some idea of one way in which such continuing identity could be achieved. In the idea presented there, experiences, thoughts and actions are seen as possessing an electrical reality which accumulates during each existence. This data is in code form and results in the creation of each personality in electrical terms. When physical death occurs, the electrical reality would still be retained.

But psychologically speaking, some allowances would also have to be made. This could be taken care of through what Seth calls the inner ego, a conscious inner counterpart of the ego with which we are familiar in daily life. The subconscious, according to this theory, acts as a buffer zone between the inner and outer ego. The inner ego contains memory of our previous lives, and acts as an overall director of activities. The subconscious sifts some information through from the inner ego (the inner self) to the outer ego. In practical terms each ego is conscious, but the outer ego is not aware of the inner ego.

Memories of past lives would not be handled by the outer ego, simply because this ego is too concerned with daily life in a physical reality to deal with extra information. The outer ego does not even concern itself with previous memories from this life. The idea of inner and outer egos is somewhat similar to the conception of secondary personalities held by psychologists. It is also rather simple to find an analogy from everyday life to explain it in easily understood terms.

As you, yourself, take on a variety of roles now as parent, mate, community member and social individual and still remain the same person, in similar fashion the inner ego would take on reincarnational roles and still retain identity and direction. At times, in your role as breadwinner, you may forget your role as a social individual or as mate, and then pick it up again at the end of the day when you return home from work. In the same manner, you would largely lose sight of other reincarnational roles while you concentrated on the one in progress. Actually, all this would involve is a change of focus. According to Seth: consciousness is the direction in which the self looks.

According to this theory, blocking of communication between the inner and outer ego was necessary in man's early evolutionary development, when all energy and attention were needed for survival on a daily basis within physical reality. Now the outer ego may be strong enough to handle such inhibited information and, indeed, may actually need it to survive in a universe which now seems to demand all its resources and knowledge. It is possible that we have blocked out previous life memories in a series of self-induced hypnotic blind spots, even as in normal existence we see only what we want to see, and block out other stimuli.

If this is the case, then we should expect to find some clues that would at least hint at the existence of past lives, clues that we have either ignored or misinterpreted. Do we have any such clues? Can the theory of reincarnation give any logical answers to questions that have tantalized the mind of man for centuries, questions for which we have several possible answers, but none that seem truly adequate?

How many times have you felt an instant like or dislike for a particular individual upon meeting him for the first time? Psychology explains this reaction in several ways. For one thing, we react in the present according to our past experience, which is partially based upon subconscious and illogical preferences or prejudices.

For example, a favorite uncle may have smoked a particular brand of cigar years ago, in your childhood. You may then be predisposed to like men who smoke that particular brand of cigar in the present, without ever realizing the connection. This is a simplified version of the way in which we actually do form prejudices and preferences. It is possible to carry this further, however, and it is just as logical actually to suppose that we sometimes take instant likes and dislikes to various persons because we have known them in some past life. We might also feel a desire to "make up" to a personality for wrongs we might have done him in a previous existence, without ever consciously being aware of either the past life or the incident involved.

Reincarnation is also interesting as a theory when it is considered along with personality tendencies and those unique interests and quirks that characterize us all. One friend of ours is intensely fascinated by Russian history, music, geography and literature. There is no apparent reason for his predisposition to study Russian life. It is possible, of course, that some forgotten childhood incident is responsible. It is also possible, however, that in some past life our friend lived in Russia.

Robert has always been intrigued with the study of old ships. His library, much of it gathered before his marriage, is filled with books concerning ships of the eighteenth century. Again this interest does not seem to be based on his background. No one else in the family knew anything about ships. He did not live as a child near the seashore nor by a harbor where his surroundings might cause such an interest. It could be explained as resulting from some incident that he has consciously forgotten. It could also be explained as a past life interest. Seth states, for example, that in his last existence Robert traveled often by ship, particularly between England and Boston, Mass.

You, yourself, may have similar tastes and preferences that you have not been able to explain, or for which you can find no apparent reason. These may be clues that can be used to give you some idea of previous interests or occupations in a possible past life. At least they should be considered.

The reincarnation theory offers an excellent explanation for the existence of geniuses and child prodigies. Talents and achievements from one life would not be lost. When a child shows great gifts early in his development—gifts that a child would not normally display—these could be the result of knowledge and ability gained in a past existence. There is an engaging economy in this concept. A small but consistent hobby in painting might result in a very real artistic talent in a next life, for example. No ability would be lost, and no action meaningless.

A sense of continuity and identity would not be consciously available to us, obviously, under most circumstances, but instead would operate as the psychic framework in which our present personalities continue their existence. In much the same manner, the child you were is alive but hardly conscious in your adult self. The child that you were is not dead. He has become something else, the adult personality. He was not a thing, but a becoming. You cannot find the child that you were in any physical place. Yet to some extent you are still the child that you were, even though you have only a glimmering of conscious memories that serve to connect you with him. In the same fashion the personality that you were in a past life may not be dead either. It may exist within you as the child does, intangible but vital, part of a psychic framework that contains and forms your present identity.

We know too little about too many things to discount such a possibility as foolish or meaningless. We do not know enough about the human personality as it exists in the present to be able to say what it was or was not in the past. Even our idea of time itself is changing.

Is it possible that in dreams we see glimpses of our past environments, streets and places that we knew in previous lives? We do know that in dreams we visit places that we knew as children. To all intents and purposes we walk down streets known to the children we once were, even though the children and the streets may exist in physical terms no longer. When this is taken into consideration, it does not seem so unlikely after all that dreams could also bring up glimpses of possible past life experience.

Do you often return to the same locations in dreams, locations with which you are not familiar in waking life? These could be scenes which were once as much a part of your daily life as the street on which you now live. It is at least conceivable that the house which you now call home could turn up in dreams in some future life to become one of those recurring dream locations that seem so strange and alien.

In dreams the self seems to wander, at least psychologically speaking, relatively free from its usual physical environment. It experiences episodes concerned with people and places which may no longer have any physical reality. Symbolism is known to be a strong element in the language of the subconscious. Such symbols are significant to the subconscious but not necessarily to the conscious mind. Looked at in this manner, it is easy to see that many seemingly meaningless dreams could be explained, if the basic symbols were discovered. These symbols would vary, however, with each individual. It is at least possible that some of these key symbols could refer to past life experience.

The Seth Material contains some evocative discussions concerning dreams, key dream symbols, and reincarnation. Here dreams are seen as containing information concerning past, present and future, with the key symbols so cunningly chosen by the inner ego that the same symbols make sense to all layers of the subconscious. One symbol, then, could refer to events from the present life, and to events of a past life, at the same time that it also held meaning for the future.

Here is an example of the way in which such dream symbols may work, so that information concerning a past existence is recalled when needed, and within the dream framework welded onto present concerns. One night I had the following two brief dreams. First of all I saw myself as a very old woman. In this dream I knew that I had cancer but I worked up until the day of my death, seemingly unconcerned. The second dream was a rather simple one in which I saw an archaic old ship that had developed a leak.

According to the Seth interpretation, the main or key symbol uniting the dreams was "tub." This symbol on a surface level served to express present worries that one day I should grow old and "turn into an old tub." The symbol expressed the same fear on this level in the second dream, where subconsciously I compared life to an old tub or ship which was leaking (as life leaking away). Here also the symbol served to remind me of an old friend, whose last name actually was Tubbs.

This was how the key symbol was used in its simplest terms. On deeper levels the symbol, according to Seth, meant much more. The old woman was actually myself in a past incarnation, in which I had died of cancer. Tub suggested a ship here again, only this time in terms of transportation, or movement in time back to a previous life. Here it served to remind me that, despite natural worries, death was only another beginning; and if I had died once, I lived again.

The tub symbol on this subconscious level, in the second dream, represented a real ship on which Robert had crossed the Atlantic in a past life, and gave me added reassurance. Though that ship had leaked, the venture had been successful. The symbol also gave me information concerning my friend M. Tubbs in the present. Seth said that she was involved in some difficulties involving water. He mentioned the possibility that she might be pregnant, and the water bag had burst. In any case it seemed positive that water was somehow involved. Through letters, we checked with M. Tubbs. She was not pregnant, but at the time of my dream the hurricane Cleo passed directly through the Florida town where she lives, close to the coast. The family had been most concerned because the water seemed to be everywhere.

Here, the one symbol "tub" contained significance for various levels of the subconscious and involved information that pertained to past, present and future. A study of your own dream notebook may allow you to discover the key symbols in your own dreams. Under self-hypnosis tell yourself that you will recall the meaning of these symbols, or discover the symbols themselves if you cannot figure them out by reading the dreams. You may also give these suggestions, without hypnosis, just before you go to sleep at night. Then examine the various dreams, using the symbols as a key to decipher them. When you are doing your Psychological Time experiments, you may also ask your subconscious to give you information about particular dream symbols.

Also examine your dream notebook to discover if you consistently speak to the same people in your dreams— people with whom you are not acquainted in normal life. If we have lived before and if part of the self has memories of past life as it has of childhood, then it is very possible that we dream of persons whom we have known in other existences. Clues as to reincarnational pasts could be found in our dreams then, clues that could help us to recall old identities.

Instruct your own subconscious to give you the meaning of such dream experiences. Again, you may do this using self-hypnosis, Psychological Time experiments, or merely given the suggestion before falling asleep at night. If you have been successful in automatic writing or automatic speech, then ask your source for the information. The Seth Material states that proof of reincarnation can be obtained through systematic studies of the human personality through hypnosis, trance states and dissociation, along with a determined investigation of all information received. This would include the checking of all data against public records and historical documents.

Such data can only come through self-exploration. We cannot hope to prove that reincarnation is possible or impossible unless we can get information from the inner personality. And we can get that information. The question will be: Is the data valid in actual terms or is it the result of subconscious fabrication? Only a checking of the apparent facts can give us the answers.

The whole matter has quite practical significance. If we have lived other lives, then we may have abilities that were developed in the past that we are not using for various reasons. If reincarnation is a fact, then it is also possible that health tendencies have origins in past lives; that neuroses have a basis in previous life experiences; that present family relationships could be explained by other personal relationships in past lives.

Whenever visitors attend a Seth session, a brief history of reincarnational existences is always given. This usually includes past family relationships, and in many cases members of the present family are seen as knowing each other in past lives. The information that we have received concerning our own families has been psychologically sound and most helpful in practical terms.

Our own experiences lead us seriously to consider the possibility of reincarnation. It is true that our experiments have given no conclusive proof, scientifically speaking, but the results are evocative enough to lead us to continue with our investigations. Neither do we have any good evidence to suggest that reincarnation is not possible.

The old arguments against the idea no longer apply. In past centuries it was easy to discount the theory by citing our lack of conscious memories of any possible past lives. Now that we understand more about the human personality, this argument is meaningless. For it is now obvious that many memories from childhood are stored up in the subconscious. We know that we react to past events, even those which we cannot consciously recall. There is no reason why past life memories could not be repressed in the same manner.

New scientific discoveries suggest that reality is far stranger than we have supposed. Einstein himself was very interested in the investigation of extrasensory perception. Certainly the discovery of anti-matter should prepare us for the possibility of other discoveries in the world of the intangible.

In a book devoted to so many other aspects of hidden phenomena, it is difficult to give more than a very brief explanation of what reincarnation may be, how it might work, and what investigations could be carried on to test its validity. We cannot afford to ignore possibilities. We cannot afford to limit our questions or investigations to known and accepted fields of endeavor. New knowledge often comes through the back door.

Following are a few brief excerpts from the Seth Material that discuss practical questions connected with reincarnation, questions that may have risen to your minds as you read this chapter. They are from various sessions and include such discussions as sex and reincarnation, past lives and family relationships, responsibility, and debts acquired in other lives.

On Reincarnation and Sex

An excess of male lives will turn a personality sour in a feminine manner, without the inner understanding and compassion that is usually associated with the female sex. In like manner, consistent feminine personalities will turn harsh without the inner strength usually associated with the male sex. For this reason, most entities live lives as male and female.

On Personal Debts and Reincarnation

It does not follow that everyone with whom you are concerned was also involved with you in past lives. You will always meet new personalities in various existences, as well as people you have known. Many times, in fact, you solve problems that arose with certain personalities, by helping other personalities in other lives.

There are laws of a sort that govern these matters. But mark my words: all debts are paid. These debts are actually challenges to the particular personality. The word "debt" implies guilt, and such a connotation is not my intention.

The sense of original sin, however, is undoubtedly in part an inner recognition of debts of this sort, but again there is no guilt in the terms usually applied.

There are always varieties of personal problems to be worked out, but the time, place and relationship are left to choice.

The reader will have to make up his own mind as to whether or not he regards reincarnation as a possible theory, an improbable theory, or a fact of life that is not as yet scientifically proven. Those who are interested should certainly read many of the excellent books on the subject that are available. Those of you who are interested in self-investigation have at least been given some hints as to how such experiments can be conducted.

To close this chapter I am including an excerpt from a Seth session in which reincarnation is discussed in connection with a particular individual. The excerpt is an excellent example of the way in which Seth uses reincarnational material as a means to explain present personality tendencies and health problems. The insight contained

in this session is psychologically sound. The person involved had a severe stuttering problem which is discussed.

Reading the excerpt, it is easy to see how any illness
or disability could have its origin in the distant past,
where it could lie dormant until triggered into activity by
an event occurring in this life. The man referred to in the
session, the guest, was an acquaintance, hardly known
to us. At the time of the session, we had only met him
once, some seven years previously. The session was the
first not held in our own home. We rarely hold sessions
for any but close friends. This was an exception to that
rule.

Excerpts from Session 89

The man was not involved with any of you in
a past life, nor do I see him in England in any
era. Instead, the Mediterranean area of the 1500's,
and it is in this period that his present speech
impediment originated.

The impediment, beginning in this life, 1507,
represented a time when he did not speak out,
and he should have, for a man's life was at stake.
He did not speak out because of fear, and now
when he wishes most to speak, he cannot.

This can be remedied. A sense of guilt carried
throughout one lifetime is somewhat understandable. A sense of guilt enduring psychologically
since the 1500's is indeed carrying conscience
just a bit too far. He has more than made up for
the original offense, which was understandable
under the circumstances.

There was an army from another country, an
invasion. A man in this individual's company was
thought to be disloyal. This man, now present at

this session, was thought to be the disloyal member. He denied it. But when they decided that another innocent man was the culprit, a man whom he knew to be innocent, then to save his own neck he let them think the innocent man was guilty.

He paid time and time again for this. No one asked that he pay. He was even then conscientious and more bothered than most would be by his own betrayal. In his immediately previous life, he plagued himself through a useless arm, right arm, so, you see, that he could not point out again. This time the self-adopted defect is less, a mere annoyance. But such annoyance becomes a form of torture.

[Immediately after the session we were told that the individual involved does not use his right hand as most people do, but is ambidextrous.]

There is no need for this. In other ways, through constructive actions, he has more than made his way. The realization that he has more than made up for the original betrayal should result, if he takes the information to heart, in a lessening of symptoms that could result, again, in their disappearance.

And he knows the man whom he once so betrayed. He has been kind to him in this life. He has given up much in this present life for the man he once betrayed. Nor does Karma say anything about an eye for an eye, nor is there any suggestion of punishment in Karma. Karma is merely, in the physical field, the result of personal development, and represents the maturing realization that we are all psychically and physically part of all that is. When we wound, it is not another that we wound, but ourselves. We do not have to bear such scars forever. There is a time when we must, even subconsciously, forget that we have trespassed.

The personality involved here *can* express himself very well. In the 1500's he was eloquent. It is precisely because this eloquence, so persuasive, so smooth-tongued, caused his superiors to believe the accusation against the innocent man, that he now fears to use eloquence, because once he let it run away from him.

It is the present personality's desire to express himself, opposed by the subconscious memories of that past life with its fear of the effects of eloquence used without discretion, that now causes the difficulty.

The man once betrayed by the present personality is now the present personality's father. Subconsciously the father knows. And why else would he demand from a son that which no father has a right to demand? I am not implying that the father consciously intends either unkindness or revenge. The present father loves the present son. It is not the son the father would wound: it is the man that the son once was.

So, as the father pays back his old betrayer, he hurts the son, without knowing why. He cannot understand his own cruelty toward this son, or the acts which he is impelled to perform. Nor can the son, loving the father, understand either the father's small cruelties, nor his own sense of gratification received from them. He, with his conscience, welcomes the small cruelties, for they make him feel he is doing penance, and for what?

For an offense that has been paid for in full. And each small cruelty committed by the father hurts the father more, for he is bewildered by his own treatment of his son, toward whom his conscious feelings are indeed paternal.

By enduring these cruelties the present personality gains two ends. One, he does needless penance, but at the same time he strikes back by causing the father hours of remorse.

In order to give the present identity a more or less logical explanation for a symptom that is of past life origin, personalities often bring forth an actual incident in this life which can then be pointed at by the personal subconscious as a scapegoat.

[Here a particular situation is described. The incident was a trivial one, gaining importance only because of the individual's inner tensions. Seth stated that the individual would not consciously recall the particular episode, but that it was used by his subconscious as a scapegoat for stuttering, and that the stuttering in this life dated from this incident.]

Communications is a field in which the personality will be extremely successful. The personality with its set limitation to vocal communication, will find satisfaction in a field or fields where the latent desire for communication can find outlet.

[The field of electronics was suggested, a field in which the individual has training.]

The personality should leave the father's house. How can he express himself in the presence of a man whom he feels he has once betrayed? He does not owe the father more now than normal filial devotion. To seek the father's pleasure superficially or to try to please the father in fields where he has no interest, will not lead to personal development or success, and will help the father in no manner either.

The love that does exist between father and son can be best maintained and nourished when the son stands alone, and the father knows that he can do so. For the sacrifices unconsciously asked by the father, the father regrets. And the sacrifices made by the son, the son regrets.

Ruburt does not believe that a house guest should behave in any such manner as I am behaving, but then I am not the house guest. I find it a rather painful duty, self-imposed, to delve into personal backgrounds, and consider myself rather dignified to adopt the pose of a psychic Peeping Tom. But there are too few who can look within themselves with candor, and if this material does anything, it must be oriented toward knowledge, and knowledge must be applied in human terms.

CHAPTER 13

Incidents that Suggest the Survival of
 Human Personality.

Who is Malba?

The Father Traynor Episode.

Seth Really Speaks Out in Booming Tones.

An Apparition at a Seth Session.

This chapter will deal mainly with some personal episodes
that led us to accept the possibility of the survival of
human personality beyond the change which we call death.
These incidents do not offer any conclusive proof of such
survival, but they do suggest evocative questions that
demand investigation. The following chapter will discuss
the matter more thoroughly in a general manner, and
suggest experiments for the reader to try for himself.

The events with which we are concerned can be divided
into two main groups: those in which automatic speech
is involved, and those in which physical effects make
themselves known. I am including the Malba incident
simply because it is interesting in itself as an example,
though a minor one, of a personality who maintains that
it once was allied with physical matter but now exists
independently of it.

The episode was the result of an experiment that Robert
and I tried on our own, and separate from the Seth
sessions. We simply sat in the quiet living room one
evening and waited. Soon I began to speak. While the

voice was my own, the choice of words, the rhythm, pacing and inflections were not my normal ones. The voice was rather weak and petulant. Malba sounded like a shallow, rather unintelligent, but well-meaning woman.

Two sessions were actually involved, about two weeks apart. In the first, very little information was obtained except that the personality called herself Malba Brownson and said that she died in South Dakota in 1946 at the age of forty-six. The second session was much more interesting, and this is the one I am reporting here.

She spelled her maiden name, Shilcock. This is her history, condensed from the session. She grew up with an aunt and an older brother, married at eighteen and worked in a dress or textile plant of some vague description in a place that sounded like Decatur, South Dakota.

We had some trouble with the word, Decatur. It was pronounced Dek-a-tur, with the accent on the first syllable. She said that she met her husband in the plant, where he was a foreman. He died in 1962 in Marlboro, England, where he was visiting relatives. After their marriage he kept his job but ran a farm where the couple lived, outside Decatur. According to Malba, the ground was poor for farming, and her husband was not a good farmer.

They were married for twenty-eight years and had a daughter and a son. The son now lives in Los Angeles, California. She didn't seem to know where the daughter was, though she mentioned that her son had two daughters. Malba herself worked in the textile factory only a few months.

Her description of her own death was rather fascinating. It was delivered in rather flat, dry tones. According to the story she told, she died in 1946, in the kitchen of the farmhouse. She was standing at the sink, washing dishes, and looking out at the "dreary" landscape. A pickup truck was parked outside. She felt a sharp pain in her chest, and died of a heart attack.

In her fall to the floor, she broke a plate. The next thing she knew, she was running across the fields looking for help. She didn't realize that she was dead until she returned to the house, and saw her body lying in the kitchen. When Robert asked where her family was at the time, she said, "My husband and son were on the farm somewhere." Robert then asked about the daughter and was told that "she run off somewheres."

The husband remarried seven months after Malba's death, and Malba was very annoyed as she spoke about the remarriage. After the husband's death, his second wife went to California to live with Malba's son and his family. Malba was bitter about this.

Her early background, as she gave it, was not pleasant. Malba's parents were not married, and she was brought up by an aunt, who also took care of the brother. Malba was ashamed because she was illegitimate and told Robert, "It's very important to have a good name." She had no use for her own parents and did not want to speak about them.

She couldn't explain how she established contact with us, and added that she "liked us because we didn't make fun of her." When asked, she said that her husband tried growing alfalfa, wheat, tobacco and corn.

Our road map docs not list any town called Decatur in either North or South Dakota. Decatur sounds something like Dakota, however, and there could have been distortion in the name. We have tried no more experiments of this sort, except one, because we have been too busy with the Seth sessions. Also, although such sessions are interesting, they do not really add much to our knowledge in any basic manner.

There is serious question as to the city in which Malba was supposed to have lived, and this has made it almost impossible to check up on the history that she gave us. It is possible, of course, that the whole affair involved subconscious fabrication on my part. On the other hand it is just as possible that the personality was a legitimate one who had indeed survived physical death.

The next incident is somewhat more complicated, and requires a brief background explanation. A certain Father Traynor was a visitor at my childhood home over a period of many years. There were periods of time when we did not see him, as he was a member of a missionary order, and often traveled. To encourage my bent for writing poetry, Father Traynor had a habit of reading to my mother and myself from an old book of poetry. Chesterton's "Lepanto" and Gray's "Elegy in a Country Churchyard" were his favorites, and he always read these two poems to us. Very seldom did he include any others. As a reader he was dramatic and used many gestures, speaking in an odd mixture of Irish brogue and rather artificial Bostonian accent.

Just before the described episode happened, I was working on a character sketch of Father Traynor. He has been dead nearly fifteen years and I had not seen much of him for the last five years or so before his death. To my dismay, my memory was not as good as I thought it was. I could remember little about him, actually. His characteristics and mannerisms had completely vanished from my conscious mind.

It was then that I decided to read aloud the two poems he enjoyed so much, hoping that as I read them my own memory would be refreshed. At least, I thought, some of his gestures might come to mind. It was 9 A.M., a bright sunny morning. The windows were wide open. I put a fresh cup of coffee on my desk, opened a poetry anthology to the poems, and began to read.

To my astonishment, my voice boomed out literally, very deep, loud and masculine. I was completely taken by surprise. The voice swept on through the entire eight pages. I walked swiftly, pacing the floor, back and forth, as I read aloud in this unusual voice. When the last poem was finished, the voice vanished.

Had it actually been as deep and loud as it seemed to me? I had no way of telling. I was alone in the apartment. Since the whole thing was unplanned, I had not recorded it. Had the voice been Father Traynor's? Had the whole affair merely been a hallucination on my part? Had the voice merely sounded loud, deep and masculine? I decided to see if the same thing could happen again, this time while the tape recorder could give me some kind of evidence.

I picked up the book, turned the recorder on, and be-

gan again. The first few words were spoken normally,
then all at once, the booming voice took over once more.
The first performance was repeated, though on a slightly
diminished level. I felt inside the voice, as if it surrounded
me with a steady exhilarating energy.

This was only the beginning of the Father Traynor
episode. The next incident happened several months later
on a Sunday evening. We were playing the tape of the
voice for our friends, Mr. and Mrs. William Gallagher.
When we finished listening to it, Bill Gallagher asked me
to read a few lines of one of the poems, trying consciously to deepen my voice to the same degree.

As it happened, I had a severe cold. My throat was
very dry and because of my cold we had missed the previously scheduled Seth session, and I doubted that the
next one, scheduled for the following night, would be
held. However, despite the cold I said that I would try.
We wanted to see how deeply I could speak, if I really
made the effort. As soon as I picked up the book, the
Father Traynor voice took over. I had one quick clear
thought: whatever was going on, my throat would never
stand it. I simply didn't see how I could read the whole
poem, even using normal volume, my cold was too bad.
But the voice swept on. The effect was even more startling
than it had been on tape.

The room was normally lit for an evening's entertain-
ment. It was far from dark. I was seated in a rocker, with
my eyes open, reading the poem. My eyes, according to
Robert and the Gallaghers, were darker and more luminous than usual. I gestured frequently with my left hand.
Subjectively the hand felt much fatter than my other hand,
but it looked no different. The gestures were not charac-
teristically my own, however. It was a warm evening. The
windows were all open, and this deep voice boomed out
in a volume that would certainly seem impossible for my
own vocal cords.

The voice had a peculiar rhythm, like a chant. It also
possessed that rather thrilling quality that excellent speak-
ers achieve, so that their voices can be heard through
large auditoriums. Incidentally, I have had no voice

training, or acting experience. When the poem was finished, the voice disappeared. We all sat around discussing what had happened. The conversation turned to the Seth sessions. Bill Gallagher has an ulcer, and we wondered what Seth might say about his condition. A most unusual Seth session began, without plan, on the spur of the moment.

This time the Seth voice spoke out even louder than the Father Traynor voice. The deep, masculine tones were unmistakable. The exceptional volume was maintained for over two hours. The pace was very fast. Seth spoke so quickly that Robert had trouble taking notes. Several times he asked Seth to slow down his delivery.

Seth told Robert to watch my features. Unfortunately, Robert was writing as fast as he could, and he did not have time to look up and still continue with the notes. We did not have a new tape for the recorder and it was not set up for "play." Bill Gallagher sat directly in front of me. Peggy was off to one side, having a view of my profile only. Bill was positive that he saw a change in my features. Peggy, from her viewpoint, could not be sure one way or the other. Robert hardly looked up. Seth had made the remark, "Watch Ruburt's features" in a rather offhand manner several minutes before.

As Seth, I pointed to Bill and told him that his ulcer would not bother him for the rest of the evening. It had annoyed him considerably and he was drinking milk. From the time that Seth told Bill the ulcer would not bother him, the pain stopped and did not return until much later, after he and Peggy had returned home. Suggestion could have been responsible for this relief, but it was most welcome to Bill, in any case. The Gallaghers are both intelligent people. Peg is a reporter for the local newspaper, and Bill works in the advertising department there. Peggy in particular, because of her profession, is trained in observing facts, and Bill is far from being gullible.

This part of the session lasted for over an hour and a half and followed immediately the Father Traynor episode. The Gallaghers left. As soon as we were alone, the session resumed. My eyes were wide open. I sat facing Robert. We both sat at the living room table.

The following are excerpts from the notes that Robert took of the remainder of this session. Since physical effects are involved here, of which I was not aware, Robert's notes will be more effective than any explanation I could give. He reported his observations on the spot.

Excerpts from notes taken by Robert Butts

"Jane began to speak from the rocker, but uttered only a few words when she got up and took a chair at the table with me. Her eyes were wide open, dark and luminous. She was staring right at me. I felt an immediate involvement that was new in the sessions. The direct stare of her eyes was disconcerting. This effect was heightened now, because I began to feel that I noticed a change in her features.

"In trying to be objective, I can say that perhaps the change I became aware of was partly physical and partly subjective on my part. Jane's features were quite animated. Where I had not noticed any change earlier, although Bill Gallagher had, now Jane's features lost some of their feminine characteristics and became more angular and drawn, as though a masculine presence were making itself seen deliberately.

"I believe that her facial planes also seemed older to me. I felt as if I were being observed by a masculine personality through her eyes. The sense of involvement with a personality other than Jane's was quite strong. I was actually more concerned in trying to decipher what change I was observing than I was in wondering whether or not there actually was a change."

(Some more rather startling voice effects were to show themselves. The following are brief excerpts from later portions of the session. They include Robert's notes and a few comments made by Seth. Please remember that Seth refers to me as Rubert, and to Robert as Joseph.)

I never want to take too much of his energy, and you are indeed a watchdog in this respect, as is right. Nevertheless, I felt that it was legitimate to take this extra time to speak with you, since there are few occasions when Ruburt's psychic abilities and energies are sufficiently attuned so that we can work together in this manner.

I regret that you must be so involved in note taking. This evening's session, all in all, will be most beneficial to Ruburt, and to you also. I must work along the lines of his development. I cannot get around him as far as his abilities are concerned. I will not push him. We would lose in the long run.

We have been involved here in variations of the trance state, while at the same time being anxious to continue with our own material, so that the two ventures have been tied into one.

Are your hands tired from note taking?

" 'No, that's all right.'
"Actually I was very tired. It was one of those situations where it was easier to keep going than to stop and then start up again. My writing hand felt a dull fatigue. Seth/Jane sat staring at me, and smiling from so close by, as if set to go on talking forever."

I quail before your quite human limitations, and if I smile, it is not with ridicule——

" 'All right.' "

But in gratitude for your fortitude. However I suggest that you take a break.

"Through this delivery I was still aware of a change in Jane's features that I thought was probably part physical and part subjective. It was as if the Jane I know so well had taken a step away from me and allowed another personality to come forward, bringing with it some slight physical change and a much larger psychological change. . . .

". . . To my genuine amazement, Jane's voice became even more powerful. This was based on sheer strength and power. There was no hint of strain as she produced this blast. I would not have been surprised at all actually to feel the ceiling vibrate over my head as she spoke. The effect was literally stunning. I have no way of measuring the magnitude of the voice to which I was listening, other than by stating that it enveloped me."

(end of Robert's notes)

The whole episode, including the Father Traynor incident, lasted for four hours. At the end of this time, my own throat was in no way strained. In fact it was more comfortable than it had been earlier in the evening. The session was the first in which such startling voice changes occurred, although in the past some occasional, less dramatic, vocal demonstrations had been given. Since this session, however, the voice effects have happened with some frequency.

Few actual physical effects have appeared, outside of the above-mentioned apparent feature changes. One such incident is particularly worthy of mention, however. During one Seth session, a friend, William Cameron Macdonell, was positive that he saw an apparition. Later definite physical effects were observed by Bill and Robert, and the room was well lit at the time. These were the circumstances.

The apparition was seen in the doorway between the living room and the bathroom. Bill saw it so clearly that he made two sketches of it, making corrections as the session continued. It was visible to him off and on for an hour. A sixty-watt bulb lit the room during this time. I continued speaking as Seth and saw nothing. Rob was seated behind the open door, taking notes. The spot in which Bill saw the apparition was out of Robert's vision entirely. He could not see the open doorway as the door itself blocked his view, nor could he leave his place at the table, since he wanted to get a verbatim account of what was said.

As Bill began sketching the apparition, I made verbal corrections as Seth.

The image in the doorway is indeed my own, though there is bound to be a distortion. It is through the inner senses that you perceive me, and this data must then be transformed into information than can be perceived by the outer senses. . . . I am a much more cheerful fellow than here portrayed. [Here, as Seth, I study Bill's sketch, looking over his shoulder.] You missed a certain cast along what you may call the cheekbones. If you watch the image more closely, I may be able to make it clearer.

There is a smugness about the lips. [Bill makes a correction in the sketch.] Ah, very good; you will find that the construction is being created by myself. Just to appear within your plane, my construction must be composed of atoms and molecules. The motion and speed of them varies from those of your regular constructions. I am, in this instance, speaking through Ruburt, while I also stand by in a construction and watch him speak. At a later date I may be able to speak from my own construction. But this will take training and I will need cooperation.

It is true that I am in some ways no beauty in your terms, yet you will attest that I am not altogether ugly. The image is a reconstruction of what I am. It represents the appearance that these abilities of mine take when at all closely connected with the physical plane. This does not necessarily mean that within all fields I have the same image.

Now during all this time, Bill kept watching the apparition. Robert's view was blocked by the door. I saw nothing as myself. During our rest period, we discussed what had happened. I confess that I was highly skeptical. I thought that perhaps Bill had imagined that he saw the apparition, that it was a hallucination. In this case, of course, I couldn't then explain Seth's comments. But since I had seen absolutely nothing, it was difficult to just take someone else's word that an apparition did appear. I had no reason to distrust Bill and felt guilty at doubting the validity of an effect of which he was absolutely certain. But during the break, I started to laugh and joke. This is when the second effect occurred, one I find most difficult to explain. I stood in the open doorway. We had turned still another light on and the room was well lit. "Is this where you saw your man in the doorway?" I laughed.

I stood within three feet of Robert and Bill. Both of them had an excellent view of my face. Suddenly, according to their account, a set of features entirely unlike my own settled down just in front of my face. They hung forward, almost transparent, with my own features visible beneath them. The features were masculine.

I didn't realize that anything had happened until both of them stared at me incredulously. Robert told me to stand still. I felt a slight tingling sensation, but that was all. When Robert and Bill compared notes, their observations agreed perfectly. Then Robert asked me to step out of the doorway. As I did, the effects instantly vanished.

To me there is no doubt at all that the physical effects actually happened. Because the features were observed by both Robert and Bill in good light, this seems to point toward the validity of the apparition also. Bill gave us two sketches that he drew of the apparition, and they remain in our files. It is highly difficult to see how these physical effects could be of subconscious origin. Had they occurred in dim light or in half darkness, their validity would certainly remain under serious question. The longevity of the apparition and the fact that the room was well lighted served to make the whole episode most intriguing.

The apparition and the feature effects appeared in a session in which Seth was discussing the nature of physical matter. According to Seth, both materializations were meant as demonstrations to point out the validity of his arguments. His main thesis, mentioned earlier very briefly, is that physical matter is constructed subconsciously by each individual, human or otherwise, within the physical system or field. As we are not aware of each breath we take, so we are not consciously aware of our own continuous construction of physical matter. On a subconscious basis, therefore, we would create and maintain our own physical images. To show how matter is constructed, Seth demonstrated with the apparition.

Incidentally, as a demonstration, the apparition and the feature effects, taken together, were quite effective, tied in as they were with the subject material of the session.

These circumstances, and others which will be related in a later chapter, lead us to suppose that the human personality does indeed possess abilities beyond those usually assigned to it. These abilities appear to be inherent within the personality whether or not it is operating within the bounds of physical matter. There may be more orthodox explanations that would involve us in fewer problems and less complicated questions, but such conventional explanations may actually hold us back from any understanding of such episodes, because they block us from looking elsewhere for answers.

The out-of-body experiences that Robert and I have both had also led us toward the belief in the basic independence of personality from the physical image. These incidents, some mentioned earlier in this book, force us to enlarge our concept of reality. If the personality in this life can detach itself from its image and travel to other physical locations, then it is not at all illogical to suppose that it can exist without the image after physical death.

How can such apparitions occur? How can the personality be independent of physical matter and to what degree? Is your own personality now independent of physical matter? In the following chapter, we will discuss these questions and look for clues that may allow us to glimpse the basic reality that is behind the physical universe. The chapter will also contain some experiments for the reader.

To close this chapter, here are some excerpts from the thirty-fourth Seth session in which Seth describes his own reality and structure.

To say I am energy is no lie. It is actually truer than many designations that would sound more authentic and complicated. I am a personality in essence-energy form. This in no way implies that I am a "spirit," some sort of a granddaddy-long-legs of science fiction. What I am is difficult to explain because of the limits set not only by your own knowledge but by the present method of our communication. . . .

I do have a structure nevertheless, and I can change or interchange the components of that structure so as to appear or operate under vastly different conditions. During these sessions I use my basic energy components in a manner other than I would under other circumstances. In other words, I can change the alignment of my components, focusing my powers into one particular direction.

If *you* wanted to enter a small space, you would, I presume, get down on all fours, hunch your shoulders and crawl into this imaginary hole head first. This would involve manipulations of muscles that would result in a temporary change of shape, a somewhat superficial but real adjustment of the physical body in its relation to space, and a consequent change of focus or direction insofar as the forward low thrust of the body into the hole.

On a much different level, this is what is involved as far as I am concerned in my attempts to enter your small entryway. On my part, however, the necessary manipulations amount to a transformation, and I have much greater freedom here. It is as if you could actually make your body smaller than the hole you wished to enter, in a much more appreciable fashion.

I have at my command boundless energy, but so have you. The main difference is that I am more equipped to draw upon this energy, and I am better equipped because I have additional knowledge which I have put to use.

Your scientists know that all matter is composed of the same elements. . . . Through methods that I have described, I can change my form. You have seen water turn to steam. This is a very simple analogy. I exist as energy, I exist electronically and sometimes chemically. I have said that I can change the alignment of my components. If I am to be considered a spirit, then all energy must be spirit.

Your idea of a spirit, I believe, is something without a form, and I can have form. I certainly have structure. It is true at this point that under ordinary circumstances you cannot see my structure. This does not mean that I have none. At some time you may be able to experience my structure. [This was before the session in which the apparition appeared.] You see, the inner senses provide direct experience. The outer senses provide camouflaged distortions of translated, second-hand experience.

You or your scientists are simply not aware yet of many basic laws that govern such things as my structure, though already some of these are glimpsed by the more original thinkers.

"In this country?"

Abroad. A few in your country are becoming aware on a very faint theoretical basis, when they consider the possibilities involved in the breaking down of physical components into basic energy forms, such theories being considered, I believe, along with a future space program.

This idea will help you understand what I mean when I say that I have structure, but can change it. I bring about such realignment of molecular patterns through direct manipulation. This will not be possible at your level. Even in the distant future such realignments will involve costly, complicated, and almost impossible achievements, because you will approach the problem working from the outside inward. The solution lies in manipulations made upon structures from the inside, or a very direct manipulation of the whole self.

Excerpts from Session 21

The designations "spirit," "medium," and so forth, are ridiculous to begin with. You are simply using your inner senses. These senses are not magical. They certainly are not religious in the usual sense of that word, and I am not some degenerating secondary personality of Ruburt's. Nor will I be compared with some long-bearded, beady-eyed spirit sitting on cloud nine.

It is simply a fact that I have lived as a human being. This meeting and other meetings are not seances, according to the implications usually given. So-called seances, when they are legitimate, are simply exercises in the use of the inner senses. The cults that have built up about such happenings are ludicrous, and in some cases unforgivable demonstrations of stupidity by well-meaning but imbecilic personalities.

Superstition breeds superstition. As far as Jane's, or Ruburt's, subconscious is concerned, I make contact with you through both of your subconsciousnesses; but through that larger portion which actually exists between planes or fields, which is the property of the mind, not the brain, and which deals with the inner senses. I have absolutely nothing to do with that portion of the subconscious which is involved with your personal memories or present personality make-up.

You asked me why this material was being given to you. My answer is, beside my strong affection for you both, that you are unaffiliated with any cult, religion, particular school of thought. You are open-minded, and not fools; not ready to cast me in the guise of pot-bellied cupid, Buddha, God, saint or devil. Such people are difficult to find.

CHAPTER 14

The "Spirit World" and the Survival of Human Personality.

Dependent and Independent Apparitions.

One evening some friends, Mr. and Mrs. J, visited us. The conversation turned to ESP. Mr. J told us that he could sometimes see the human aura—subtle emanations thought by some to surround the body like a halo. He insisted that he could see his wife's aura, even as we sat chatting together. I had never seen an aura; however, I was willing to accept the possibility that they might exist.

Curious, I decided to try a little experiment. I told Mr. J that I would concentrate on his wife's aura (though I couldn't see it) and try to make it rise higher above her head. He agreed to tell me whether or not I succeeded. Instead, without telling anyone, I concentrated on trying to make the aura brighter. After a minute or so passed, Mr. J told me that the aura wasn't rising, but that it was getting brighter in intensity.

I have to admit that I was somewhat astonished. We then decided to conduct another small experiment. The room was fairly well lighted. An ordinary living room lamp was burning. We sat together, in the same corner by the lamp, and held hands. I asked, "Is there anyone here?" Almost at once Mrs. J yelled out, "Someone grabbed my hand." At the same time, her hand broke contact with mine and shot into the air. Her elbow was pressed tightly to the coffee table, with the hand held stiffly upward and the fingers slightly curved, as if they were in contact with other fingers. From the rigidity of the muscles of her arm

214

and hand, and the tension, it seemed as if a weight pressed down upon them. Mrs. J was shaking and perspiring profusely. None of us could see anything unusual, however, except for Mrs. J's behavior.

She kept insisting that someone invisible had grabbed hold of her hand, and was pressing down upon her arm. She was obviously frightened. Again, though the room was well-lit, we saw nothing. Mrs. J certainly wasn't acting. Tears began to run down her cheeks. I didn't know if a personality was present and invisible to us, or if the young woman was highly suggestible.

In a firm voice, I said, "You will let Mrs. J's hand go, and leave us alone." I repeated this several times, knowing that if Mrs. J were overly suggestible, then this countersuggestion would remove the difficulty. On the other hand, if an invisible personality were present, it was being asked to leave us, and I hoped in this instance that it would then do so.

As soon as I spoke the words, her hand slammed down on the table top, making a loud noise that startled all of us. We all jumped, and looked about the room. I kept repeating, "You will leave us now. You will let the young woman alone," until Mrs. J quieted. Because of her state of nerves, I did not think it advisable to continue. As a result, no conclusions were reached at all. Mrs. J did not feel comfortable for the rest of the evening. If a survival personality were present, it certainly was an active one.

This brings us to several points concerning such experiments in general. I suggest that no such seances be held in darkness. While I can offer no proof, it seems to me that any personality who has survived physical death will not be annoyed by a small matter of lights. Darkness of itself breeds suspicion and inflames imaginations. Mediums have long insisted upon darkness, and this one demand has hampered the investigation of psychic societies as much as anything else. In your own experiments, keep the room fairly well lit. The atmosphere can still be restful and intimate. Had the above mentioned experiment been conducted in darkness, it could have frightened the young woman to a much greater degree than it did.

This is the only incident in any of our experiments that was at all unpleasant. It is important that those taking part in such episodes use common sense and emotional integrity. Those conducting such experiments need a strong sense of responsibility in maintaining the proper atmosphere, conditions, and attitude. We do not know enough yet about suggestion itself or the personality in general to take chances. At any signs of uneasiness on the part of anyone participating, the sessions should immediately be ended.

It is possible that suggestion does play an important part in such proceedings; yet suggestion itself must be controlled. It may be used, but not encouraged to run wild. Obviously if the possibility of invisible personalities were not accepted at all, there would be no point in such experiments. So the acceptance of this possibility in itself sets up a suggestion before the session is even begun. It is not true, therefore, to say that suggestion plays no part in these proceedings. Suggestion is important in every aspect of our lives, in these experiments as well as in any other area. But if you are seeking legitimate results you should not let your imagination run away with you either.

It is also possible that an invisible personality might operate in some sort of emotional manner in ways we do not understand. In conducting experiments of this sort, it is up to you to maintain an equilibrium. Personally I do not suggest that you attempt to get in touch with personalities with whom you or your friends have been closely connected, unless you are extremely level-headed. In such a case the emotional stress might become so strong it would be difficult to be objective either about the experiment itself or about its results.

More about such experiments will be said later in this chapter. Before we discuss the survival of the human personality, however, let us consider the personality as we know it in ordinary existence; and before we attempt to discuss the so-called spirit world, let us look more closely at our own present subjective experience.

Actually how physical is our usual experience? How much of our reality exists within physical matter now, and how much of it exists in a reality that we can neither see nor touch? As a species we are composed of organic tissue, but in many ways our reality seems to have its being in some medium other than flesh and bone.

None of us would deny the reality of our thoughts, for example, yet a thought is not a physical object like a glass that we can hold in our hands. When we try to examine a thought, we instantly change it. The original thought vanishes, to be replaced by a new one. We can only know what a thought is through our own inner experience.

Neither would we deny the validity of psychological insights or emotions or dreams. These are in no way concrete objects, yet they form an important part of our own consciousness. Such subjective experiences seem to be connected with physical matter, but they do not seem to be literally contained within it.

We say that dreams exist "in our heads." But certainly dreams are not in our heads in the same manner that physical tissue and blood vessels and bones are in our heads. A surgeon can probe into our brain tissue with a scalpel, but no physical examination or operation will disclose a dream or a thought or a psychological experience. No scalpel can cut into a dream as it can pierce the visible fibers inside our bony skulls. Then what do we actually mean when we assume that dreams and thoughts are inside our heads?

The idea is based on the assumption that the human personality is limited by physical matter and held in bounds by the physical self. Therefore, anything belonging to the personality would have to exist within the physical organism. If we are purely physical creatures, then, we would still have to admit that we contained some things that were not physical, otherwise these thoughts and dreams inside of us would have to be physical also, and they are not.

Scientists have theorized that consciousness may be the result of the ways in which the body operates. Even if this were the whole story, and I do not believe it is, then we would still have to admit that part of our reality was not physical, but was born out of physical matter and could not be seen and touched. Nevertheless, because of this attitude we have the idea that reality is determined by physical existence only. We consider valid only those things which can be judged so by the physical senses.

It seems to make no difference that physicists have discovered that the senses themselves distort reality, and that we merely create patterns out of atoms and molecules, perceive these as objects and give them names. In general we still act as if physical reality were the only standard by which to measure experience.

We can hardly refer to something which affects us deeply as unreal. We can say that an experience exists in some perspectives and not in others. Many dreams are as vivid and valid as any waking experience, for example, and have as great an effect upon our personalities. The dream may not have a physical reality but it certainly has a psychological reality.

Let us consider how real or unreal various experiences are. Take the locations that appear to us in dreams. It is true that dream locations do not exist within our heads in the same way that physical streets exist within the spaces of cities. While we are within the context of a dream, however, the location appears to be immediate. In dreams we may walk down avenues which do not exist in physical terms. We receive data we would call sensual if we were awake. We hear, touch, taste, smell, and operate in a manner that we would call physical if we were awake. We walk, talk, act, work, play, while our actual bodies are at rest.

I can find Water Street at any time I choose: for all practical purposes it is a permanent feature of the city of Elmira, in which I live. But I cannot return to a dream location any time I choose. Can we say, then, that dream locations are different from physical places in that we cannot return to them? Not quite, since in recurring dreams many of us do visit the same streets and houses with which we have become familiar in other dreams. If we cannot find dream locations when we are in the waking state, neither can we find physical locations when we are dreaming. There is good reason to suppose that we can return to various dream locations simply by suggesting that we will do so before we go to sleep. So the dream world may possess an organized structure also, just as the physical world does, and one in which we all know our way very well—while we are sleeping.

Such matters may at first seem far divorced from a discussion of the so-called spirit world. However, perhaps you can now see that we are much more than creatures composed of physical matter. Our intimate direct experience transcends physical reality as we know it. We are a mixture of corporeal substance and something else that we can only approach through subjective experience, a something that makes us what we are, and without which consciousness would be meaningless.

Consciousness is precisely that part of ourselves which does not exist as an object within the physical universe, and it is composed of those thoughts and emotions and dreams in which we realize ourselves most intimately. It makes no difference what you call this portion of our personalities, spirit, or soul, or mind. The point is that the most vital aspects of the self are not physically materialized.

It is true, however, that clues to the existence of this portion of the human personality can be found in physical matter. Our emotions can be tampered with through the addition or subtraction of chemicals and hormones. To some extent our personalities can be manipulated. Even a subtle alteration in physical make-up will effect a change in our inner selves. But the fact remains that very significant experiences upon which our consciousness and identities depend are not physical in the usual terms.

If this reality of ourselves is not contained within matter but only connected to it, then it is quite legitimate to say that we operate and exist in both physical and non-physical dimensions. At times we are more closely allied with the corporeal universe than at other times. In dreams, for example, we are less closely bound to the physical world than we are in the waking state. Our sensual apparatus is turned down low, to the idling stage. We are maintained within the physical universe, but we limit our operations within it. It becomes as unreal to us as the dream state becomes when we are awake.

It is at least conceivable that the *I* of our dreams is but another aspect of our own identity; an *I* of which we are largely unaware in our waking hours; an *I* that continues now to exist as itself despite the ego's manipulation of the physical universe; and an *I* that will continue to exist after the alliance with physical matter is finished.

Psychologists' studies of secondary and multiple personalities show that it is very possible for one self to contain several other personalities, each unaware of the other, each functioning under various situations, and all expressing diverse abilities and attitudes. The dreaming self and the waking self are parts of the same personality, each functioning under different circumstances. The concept of the inner and outer egos, as Seth calls them, gives quite plausible explanations to several of our questions. The inner ego, operating within dreams, would not be dependent upon physical matter for its consciousness nor identity. On physical death, this inner self would simply continue to act as it had done before—perhaps by becoming the dominant part of the personality while the outer ego then operated in the same manner as the subconscious does in this existence.

Human personality is more complex than we imagine. Your own experiments, since beginning this book, should have already allowed you to become aware of abilities and perceptions of which you possibly were not aware. Through your own experience thus far, you may now realize that the conscious ego is merely the part of the whole self that functions within physical matter. But the portion of the personality that includes the subconscious, the dreaming *I*, is not so bound and appears to perceive realities with which the outer ego is unfamiliar, and to operate under conditions in which the waking self would falter.

The question is not: Is there a spirit world? The question is: What is the nature of this part of the human personality which is even now partially independent of physical matter? What are its potentials and limitations and characteristics? Perhaps most important of all, does this part of the self continue to exist when the alliance with physical matter is ended?

For if we are even partially independent of the physical system now, then there is nothing illogical in supposing that the personality, in whole or part, may continue to exist. The self is not a concrete object. It is forever changing. The experience of death would change it, as any experience does. As we cannot predict the effect of any event on any given personality, so we cannot predict the manner in which death would alter the living individual consciousness.

We do know that consciousness would no longer be physically oriented. It should be remembered here that at least a third of each twenty-four hour period is spent in sleep, when we do not operate in an ego-directed manner, oriented toward physical reality, but in a subconscious intuitive fashion focused toward inner subjective reality. The clues to explain the behavior of the personality after physical death could well be found by a systematic examination of the personality's behavior during the sleep and trance states. For this *I* of the sleep state would have to be the part of us that would survive —the subjective *I* which is already somewhat independent of physical matter.

A study of our own dream records over a period of two and a half years vividly suggests that the personality is far from disorganized in sleep. The inner logic, intuitions and dream constructions show complexity, variety and purpose. This is not the chaotic scramble state thought to be associated with the dreaming self.

It is very possible that human personality, if it survived physical death, would show some of the characteristics that are displayed by the present personality in periods of dreaming, trance and other dissociated conditions. At such times, there is a definite consciousness, and consciousness of self. On occasion there is even an ego awareness, but the borderlines between the levels of the personality are not as definite as they are in the waking state.

Certainly the imagination and creative aspects of the personality are given greater play in the dream state. Problem-solving seems to follow the line of intuitive play-acting, rather than the reasoning process. In dreams, for example, we solve problems by constructing dream dramas in which we act out various solutions. The actual dreams and the discarded solutions are often consciously forgotten, yet on many occasions we waken with the problem solved for us. Such dream work suggests that the sleeping personality may not lack its own kind of direction, purpose and order. It is possible that the personality after physical death may display the same kind of inner activity.

We have long known that mind influences matter, but we have not known how or to what extent. Even the words themselves, "mind" and "matter," have changed. The Seth Material presents the idea that physical matter is constructed by all living things, on a subconscious basis. (Individuals of other species are seen as having a generalized consciousness rather than an organized ego. Their state of awareness would be compared to our subconscious state.) According to this theory, the ego is as unaware of this continuous creation of physical matter as it is of the constant birth and rebirth of the atoms within the physical stuff of its own image. The concept is fully developed although it can only be discussed briefly here. The theory includes detailed explanations of the manner in which agreement is reached as to the placement of objects in space.

The idea is not at all far-fetched when it is considered along the lines of current discoveries in the field of physics. If this is the way in which physical matter is constructed, then at physical death the individual would simply cease this subconscious construction of his own physical image. The personality would continue to exist. The inner self would remain a psychological unit, although the ego might no longer operate as a dominant part of the self.

It would be possible, then, for the personality under

certain conditions to re-form an approximation of his original physical self, appearing to us as an apparition. It is conceivable that the personality's command over physical matter would not be as effective as it had been and that the molecular structure might be faulty. The ego would not have disappeared, but would have been assimilated by the rest of the self upon physical death. It would, in the instance of an apparition, momentarily return to its old position as a director of psychological activity. Again, the control over physical matter would not be as efficient under these conditions, but it could under some circumstances be adequate enough to make a materialization obvious to the senses of an observer.

It would also theoretically be possible, then, for such a personality to make itself known in one way or another by expressing itself through the physical image of another personality who was still operating within our system. In this case a cooperation of sorts would be maintained, a psychic or psychological working relationship between the two personalities. A medium would then be a person who allows such cooperation to exist. In these circumstances, no independent apparition would be formed, but the "free" personality would be permitted to use the vocal cords or other portions of the medium's involuntary muscular apparatus.

An independent apparition would be one who utilizes physical matter to form a free-standing image of its own, an image that might or might not be faulty by our standards. A dependent apparition would be able to communicate only through the temporary cooperation of an individual already operating within the physical system. A dependent apparition would only be able to make itself known through the changes it could effect in the behavior of the other personality who cooperated with it.

As far as I know, this theory and the classification of apparitions is original, developing out of my own thoughts and experiences. I am certain, however, that any spirit world, world of mind, or whatever you prefer to call it would not be unfamiliar to us. For one thing, it would already exist within the physical matter of which we are composed, and perhaps be that illusive characteristic that gives life to physical matter itself. The unconscious or subconscious would already have inner awareness of this reality. Only the ego would find it unfamiliar.

Again, clues as to the nature of this reality could be discovered by examining our own awareness now, as it is inner-directed rather than outer-directed. The Psychological Time experiments listed earlier in this book will allow you to dissociate yourself to some degree from the ego's intense focus upon the physical environment, so that some awareness of this inner reality can be experienced. A study of the dreams listed in your own notebook will acquaint you with the inner order of the personality that exists behind the seemingly chaotic nature of dream actions. All of the experiments in this book will allow you to achieve greater flexibility.

As you progress, the ego will gradually become aware of its relationship with other portions of the whole self. Because it is taken into consideration in our experiments, it will be more willing to step aside momentarily so that the focus of awareness can be turned to other areas of reality in which it is not equipped to function effectively.

We have already mentioned independent and dependent apparitions. In your own experiments some important factors must be taken into consideration. There are definite problems concerned with any possible communications with apparitional personalities, and some of these should be more thoroughly discussed.

It is highly difficult to prove the validity of apparitional communication, communication which is allegedly established with personalities who have survived physical death. For one thing, even if the data is legitimate, we often take it for granted that such personalities operate in the same manner as we, and this, I believe, is a mistake. Their psychological structure may have altered in some respects; the ego, for example, may not be as necessary to a non-physical being. The ego is extremely specialized, geared toward material orientation.

It is most probable that such personalities would display instead characteristics of consciousness with which we have become familiar in dream, trance and other dissociated states. Communication would be more associative, intuitive and symbolic than that which appertains to the waking state. We can hardly suppose that the psychological structure of a personality who has survived physical death is the same as our own. We cannot, therefore, expect that communication will follow the lines which are familiar to us. To expect this is asking too much, and may lead us in the wrong direction.

The communications problem confronted by an apparitional personality would be far greater than the effort needed on our part to perceive the communication. Such a personality would have to impress a physical system in which it no longer operates. For an independent apparition, atoms and molecules would have to be built up to form a fairly consistent image. A certain minimum muscular system would have to be constructed, and so forth. It should be remembered here however that this is precisely what we do, though not consciously, as we grow from infants to adults. We add to the physical matter that composes our image. We build, maintain and develop our body. An independent apparition would do the same thing but from scratch.

A dependent apparition would not face nearly so many problems. It would merely manipulate already constructed matter, working through some kind of psychological cooperation with a living individual. In this case, however, there might be some distortions from the subconscious areas of the individual still within the physical system.

Your "Ouija" board experiments may give you excellent instances of this. If you receive a message that claims to originate with such a personality, get as much information as you can, bearing in mind that your source may not be concerned with our kind of facts. Mental events, for example, might be considered quite legitimate facts by the communicator, while you may not think them facts at all. Also, time is relative and in apparitional reality, time, as we know it, may have no meaning.

In other words, a communicating personality may experience time in the same way that we do when we are in states of dissociation. This is not the continuous time system with which we are familiar, and we may have to make some adjustments in this respect when dealing with information containing a time element.

There are standards against which to measure your own messages, whether received through the "Ouija" board, automatic writing, automatic speech or through other procedures. They were noted earlier in this book, and it is vital that you consider them when judging such communications. It is also possible that valid data may be concealed in material that is mainly of subconscious origin. If this is the case, then continued experimentation may lead to a gradual weeding out of personal data with an accompanying rise of valid information.

With a dependent apparition, the personality most likely would make his entry through the subconscious of the person experimenting, affecting the autonomic nervous system and involuntary muscular system. In the case of a "Ouija" board, for example, this would result in the movement of the pointer. An independent apparition would have greater freedom, at least theoretically, though it is more than possible that there are important psychological connections on an emotional level that affect even an independent apparition. This connection could operate between the observer and the apparition.

Automatic writing could also be used as a method of communication by a surviving personality. In this case the apparition would be a dependent one, as with the "Ouija" board. Automatic speech is the method I am most familiar with. So far I have had no success with automatic writing. My suspicion is that my ego has set up barriers in this respect, since I am a writer by profession. The ego, in other words, wants credit for its own productions. Speaking for Seth does not bother me in this way, although if I had been in the habit of dictating when I wrote, then perhaps barriers would also have been erected against automatic speech.

Such communications raise as many questions as they answer. Until further investigations are carried on in these areas, we can give no conclusive evidence as to their origins. We can say that the communications are not conscious ones. Neither do the best of them seem to be of subconscious origin, unless the term subconscious itself be broadened to include more than it does at present. I am speaking now of material of highest quality, not of communications that are obviously subconscious fabrications. Certainly such phenomena seem to point toward the existence of personalities who have survived death, and indicate an inner reality that resides within the framework of living matter—a reality that continues to exist independently of the corporeal framework in which it once found expression.

It will help if you expand your own reading to include books that deal with ESP. Many cases of spontaneous apparitions are documented, but they cannot be discussed in this book, which deals with so many other aspects of psychic phenomena. I would, however, recommend that you look for such material in your public library, and a suggested reading list is included at the end of this book.

Question your own acquaintances as to any apparitions they may have seen, or thought that they saw. Several people of my acquaintance have told me about such experiences. We cannot take it for granted that all "apparition sightings" are the result of overworked imaginations or subconscious projection.

If it is finally accepted that the personality in whole or part survives death—and I believe that it will be—then such a belief will be considered as modern as a belief in spaceships and rockets. For centuries men scoffed at the idea of travel to the moon. Today such seemingly impractical dreams are realities that affect our daily lives, our national economy, education and politics.

Modern knowledge is opening up new fields of endeavor. We can no longer afford to hide portions of human experience in the dark closets of superstition and ignorance and pretend they do not exist. We must probe realistically into all aspects of existence and explore new and old theories with open-minded speculation, imagination and reason.

Evidence of inner reality can be searched for in all of

the previous experiments given in this book. Those of you who are open-minded but not gullible may find experimental seances a most interesting method of investigation. Reread the material on this subject in Chapter Three. A simpler procedure might be used in which you merely sit with friends in a quiet room. Moderate lighting, neither too dim nor too bright, is best for your purposes. You may sit in semidarkness if you prefer, but in my opinion such sessions should be conducted in as reasonable an atmosphere as possible. You are not apt to feel inner-directed in a room blazing with lights; you should, however, be quite comfortable in moderate light. If anyone needs darkness for such experiments it is quite possible that he and not the "spirits" find darkness conducive.

Be relaxed, receptive and quiet. You may sit in a circle with the others participating if you choose, holding hands if you wish. We simply do not know enough about such matters to say whether or not certain contacts are set up through touch. Our own experience, however, does not seem to point toward that conclusion. Then simply wait. You may ask in a low voice: "Is there anyone here?"

Such experiments require common sense on the part of the participants. Discipline is essential. Overly active imagination will not yield legitimate results. It will only add to the suspicion already surrounding seances in general. On the other hand a sense of spontaneity is absolutely necessary, and a certain controlled permissiveness. Your own experiments with Psychological Time will give you experience in the change of focus that is needed here.

Always remember the importance of keeping notes on all sessions, particularly where experimental seances are involved. Those of you who have tape recorders should by all means record your sessions. Screen the participants well. They should be people who are absolutely trustworthy, open-minded and well-balanced. Naturally, they must be individuals with whom you feel comfortable. You may find that such sessions have better results with some participants than with others. Our experience certainly seems to indicate that the personalities involved have a great deal to do with success or failure.

Personally, I am convinced the human personality does survive the change which we call death. Although we have no scientific evidence of this at present, there is no reason to suppose it will always be lacking. It must be remembered that proof for the survival of the personality was, in the past, considered needless. Religions insisted upon such belief as an article of faith. It is hoped that before too long a search into such phenomena will be admitted as legitimate by our scientific communities. As discoveries in the field of physics close the gap between matter and non-matter, and as biological discoveries close the gap between living and inert matter, we may very well blunder on further knowledge that will of itself open up new possibilities.

The following excerpts from the twenty-fourth Seth session discuss the inner self and its relation to the physical universe and to nonphysical reality.

Some part of the individual is aware of the most minute portions of breath. Some part of the individual knows immediately of the most minute particle of oxygen and components that enter the lung. The thinking brain does not know. Your all-important *I* does not know.

In actuality, my dear friends, the all-important *I* does know. You do not know the all-important *I,* and therein lies your difficulty. It is fashionable to consider man, or man's *I,* as the product of the brain and an isolated bit of the subconscious, with a few odds and ends thrown in for good measure.

Therefore, with such an unnatural division it seems to man that he does not know himself. He says, "I breathe, but who breathes, since consciously I cannot tell myself to breathe or not to breathe?" He says, "I dream, but who dreams? I cannot tell myself to dream or not to dream." He cuts himself in half, then wonders why he is not whole. Man has consistently admitted to evidence only those things he could see, smell, touch or hear, and in so doing he only appreciates half of himself, and here I exaggerate. He is aware of only a third of himself, because two-thirds of himself exists in that realm which he will not admit. . . .

If man does not know who breathes within him, and if he does not know who dreams within him, it is not because there is one who acts in the physical world and one, completely separate, who breathes and dreams. It is because he has buried the part of himself who breathes and dreams. If these functions seem so automatic as to be performed by someone completely divorced from himself, it is because he has done the divorcing. . . .

I mentioned earlier that oftentimes the consciousness becomes the subconscious and vice versa. This should come as no surprise. You are familiar with this in your everyday existence. It is not some isolated occurrence that happens but once in a lifetime; and yet as a rule man has ignored this fact completely. In sleep the conscious actually becomes the subconscious, and the subconscious in a very real manner, becomes conscious. Every man instinctively knows this, and yet every man stubbornly refuses to admit it.

The part of you who dreams is the *I* as much

as the part of you that operates in any other manner. The part of you who dreams is the part of you who breathes. And this part is certainly as legitimate, and actually more necessary to you as a whole unit, than the part that also plays bridge or Scrabble. It would seem ludicrous to suppose that such a vital matter as breathing would be left to a subordinate and almost completely divorced, poor relative sort of a lesser personality.

As breathing is carried on in a manner that seems automatic to the conscious mind, so the important function of transforming the vitality of the universe into pattern units also seems to be carried on automatically. But this transformation is not as apparent to you; therefore it seems as if it were carried on by someone even more distant and alien than the unrecognized part of yourself that breathes. . . .

The facts are simply that you yourselves form these camouflage patterns [the physical world]. You form the world of appearances with the same part of you that breathes. You do not admit the breather as being a part of yourselves consciously, nor do you admit the creator of the camouflaged physical universe as being part of yourselves.

Because you know that you breathe without being conscious of the mechanics involved, you are forced, despite your inclinations, to admit that you do your own breathing. When you cross a room you are forced to admit that you have caused yourself to do so, even though you have no conscious knowledge of willing the muscles to move. And yet, even though you realize these things, you do not really believe them. In your quiet unguarded moments you still say, "Who dreams?"

Since it is so difficult for man to recognize the part of himself that moves his own muscles and breathes his own breath, I suppose that it is not startling that he cannot realize that his whole self also forms the camouflage world of physical matter, in almost the same manner that he forms a pattern with his breath upon a glass pane.

When I say that you actually create the camouflage patterns of your own physical universe yourselves, by use of inner vitality in the same manner that you form a pattern with your breath upon a glass pane, I do not necessarily mean that you are creators of the universe. I merely am saying that you create the physical world as you know it, and herein, dear friends, lies a vast tale.

Nor do I know all the answers. It is, however, a fact that even mankind, in his blundering manner, will discover that he himself creates his own physical universe, and that the mechanisms of the physical body have more functions and varieties than he knows.

CHAPTER 15

ESP Investigations in General.
Mediums and Controls.
Conclusions.

Parapsychology is a branch of psychology concerned with the investigation of evidence for telepathy, clairvoyance and the like, and with experimentation in the field of extrasensory perceptions. Parapsychologists insist that ESP is a proven fact. Men like J. B. Rhine in this country and Willem Tenhaeff of Holland, among others, have spent their entire adult lives studying ESP under strict laboratory conditions. With some notable exceptions, psychologists will often state emphatically that ESP has not been scientifically demonstrated. Those of you who have read *Croiset the Clairvoyant* by Jack Harrison Pollack will find it difficult to believe that the evidence for ESP can be doubted.

Indeed, telepathy and clairvoyance have been demonstrated under scientific conditions by Croiset countless times, and the Rhine experiments with Zenar cards also present their own evidence. Various out-of-body experiences have been documented by investigators of whose integrity there can be no doubt. Apparitions *do* appear, regardless of our dismay. Countless cases of such events are in the records of the various psychic societies.

ESP is a proven fact. We know that it exists and is part of the framework within which we operate as human beings. We do not know how it works, why it works, when it works, though we do have some partial answers to these questions. Often the very attempt to test an individual's abilities makes these abilities inoperable, at least temporarily. Success at home under familiar conditions is one thing. Success in a laboratory with the resulting tension is something else again. ESP happens spontaneously often enough. Until we know more about its characteristics we shall probably continue to have difficulties under test conditions. Luckily some psychics are gifted enough to put their abilities to practical use and allow their talents to be investigated. Professor Tenhaeff, working with Croiset, has added to our knowledge concerning ESP and its connection to the associative process of the mind.

There is no doubt that ESP abilities are more closely connected with the intuitions and the subjective self than with the logical portions of the egotistical self. One theory suggests that these abilities were much more prominent in prehistoric uncivilized man, and that they have tended to recede with the advance of evolution. It is also possible, however, that we have simply ignored them in our headlong plunge into materialism and technology.

The more pragmatic and "objective" we are, the less we use our ESP abilities. This, of course, leads us into one of our difficulties. Those who investigate ESP with a strictly pragmatic attitude are often prejudiced against it. Those who are not pragmatic are accused of lacking scientific objectivity. The ideal investigator would be an individual who was both intuitive and trained in scientific methods.

Since these abilities are subconscious rather than conscious, they show the characteristics displayed by the personality in subjective states. Often subconscious symbolism is involved. Here again Pollack's *Croiset* gives excellent examples of the importance of association (one idea leading to the next) and how it can operate to build up a clairvoyant image. Distortions occur at times, however. The language of the subconscious must be investigated. We must learn to decipher it with some precision.

The whole matter of mediums in general is one that parapsychologists and psychologists alike would probably prefer to forget, if possible. Unfortunately they cannot do so, since some excellent evidence of ESP has been received from mediums. Mental mediums are those individuals who deal primarily with mental rather than physical effects, showing clairvoyant knowledge, for example, rather than producing apparitions or moving physical objects.

Mental mediums are far easier to investigate since they do not as a rule insist upon darkness or semidarkness as conditions of operation. We simply do not know whether or not darkness will facilitate the legitimate appearance of apparitions. Darkness certainly does facilitate fraud. Personally I think that light bothers the human beings involved far more than it annoys the apparitions that may appear.

Psychologists and parapsychologists alike have been hoodwinked by fraudulent mediums in the past to such an extent that their attitude now is: guilty until proven innocent. While this may work very well for the scientists and may actually improve the quality of scientific evidence, the attitude is regrettable from other standpoints. Those who have receptive ability, or suspect that they may have, are understandably reluctant to step forth. A failure under such circumstances implies not a natural consequence of nervousness but an indication of duplicity.

Most mediums are convinced they are controlled by a personality who has survived physical death, when they are in the mediumistic trance state. This personality is called a "control." Sometimes through such seances, information is obtained that could not be known to any living persons. I am speaking now of cases where no fraud has ever been discovered. Since investigators naturally look for fraud more avidly than any detective searches out a murder suspect, this means that the medium involved is literally as pure as the driven snow.

Such performances can be explained, however, without the personality survival theory. The medium in such instances may be using her own clairvoyant abilities. It is also possible that the control personality is simply a subconscious device adopted unknowingly by the medium to allow her—or him—to use abilities in which the ego will have no part.

This would serve to protect the medium from over-concern, from distracting worries as to whether or not information was correct. A failure would not be her failure, but a failure of the control personality. When investigators watch for slip-ups like bloodhounds, this could be a most useful subconscious device to relieve psychological strain. It could also allow the intuitive elements of the self to operate separately, unrestrained by the logical dictates of the egotistical self. With some individuals, such a psychological mechanism might be necessary.

It is also possible that these control personalities are precisely what they say they are. While no survival personality has ever popped up in the middle of a parapsychologist's laboratory, many documented instances of apparitions make the prospect of personal survival more probable than is generally supposed. Further documented cases of "out-of-body" experiences would help, for if it can be proven beyond all doubt that the personality can in life appear in two places at once, then the survival thesis would be advanced. Some excellent cases have been documented, and these should not be forgotten.

The mediumistic trance, regardless of what else it is, is similar to the hypnotic trance; at least it appears to be. I do not enter the deeper trance that is usually characteristic of mediums, however, during our own sessions. Whether or not I will do so in the future remains to be seen. The trance state itself, regardless of anything else, is undoubtedly necessary simply as a method of including concentration inward and of blocking out distracting outer stimuli.

We are now beginning on our own a very simple testing procedure during the Seth sessions that we hope will enable us to see what Seth can come up with, on a fairly consistent basis, in connection with clairvoyant material. I was quite nervous on the first occasion, and can see where a deeper trance state would have allowed greater freedom. In my light trance, I can be aware of two lines of thought at once: my own and Seth's, Seth's taking precedence. Without realizing what I was doing during our first test, I switched, using two sources. The results of the test showed that Seth's information was right and my own was wrong. I make no conscious attempt to induce a trance during or before sessions but let events happen naturally. Since the deeper state has not generally occurred during sessions, we have let matters stand. The test experience taught me in one simple lesson, however, to distinguish between Seth's communications and any distortive thoughts of my own that might enter. This experience is invaluable.

The trance, whether it actually enables a survival personality to speak, or whether it is simply a handy psychological device, is extremely helpful under such conditions. Certainly psychologists and legitimate mediums should join forces in an honest effort to discover what is actually involved.

ESP investigations that do not involve mediums are far easier to evaluate. Croiset, for example, does not use any spirit control of any kind, and scientific proof of his abilities is clear. The same applies to Peter Hurkos, who now demonstrates his abilities in this country. If survival personalities do exist and communicate with the living, then the medium's control is legitimate not only from a psychological standpoint, but for quite practical reasons. Otherwise the control and the mediumistic trance itself may be basically unnecessary but psychologically important. Some individuals with great psychic abilities may not need to resort to this "artificial" personality. Others may find it an aid in maintaining overall psychological stability.

These are all questions to which we have no answers, and questions that are vital to our understanding of ESP in general. Parapsychologists and psychologists differ in their approach to such matters. The field of parapsychology is still not considered quite respectable by other scientific communities, although this attitude is now changing. Psychologists bend over backward in an attempt to be objective, and as a result they often seem to refuse to accept very legitimate evidence. While individual psychologists may be more open-minded, the tendency toward distrust of ESP seems to be characteristic of psychology in general. Psychology had to work very hard itself to prove its own scientific authenticity, and this may account for its rigidity in this respect.

The situation is felt by those individuals who have become aware of their own abilities, since the attitude of parapsychologists and psychologists toward such individuals is partially the result of the tension existing between the two groups. The first reaction in the field is "Prove it. Now." Again, there is nothing wrong in the desire of parapsychologists to prove their case. It is the only way to achieve acceptance.

In my opinion ESP has been proven to all except those who refuse to accept the evidence. What is needed now is an atmosphere of cooperation and mutual trust among parapsychologists, psychologists and those with definite ESP abilities. The "all right, show me" attitude is not conducive to such an endeavor. The human element must be considered in this field more than any other. Excellent objective demonstrations will most likely result from a friendly relationship between these groups. But ESP abilities will not operate effectively, if they operate at all, under conditions of mistrust or suspicion.

The field of parapsychology obviously cannot be all things to all people. It is to be congratulated for investigating questions that have been avoided in the past by organized searchers after knowledge. In its quest for scientific proofs, however, it is hoped that it retains in the future that spirit of adventurousness and wonder that gave it its original impetus.

The field steers clear of the problem of reincarnation also, and understandably, since it is a sticky question. Yet time and time again the subject rears its head, as with the work of the late Edgar Cayce. Cayce was a healer who in the trance state correctly prescribed treatment for ill patients, whether or not the patients made a visit to him or contacted him by mail. Hard as it may be to accept, there is no doubt that he often succeeded where medical doctors failed. In this trance state, however, he also discussed reincarnation, insisting upon it as a fact of human existence. The health readings have been proven valid.

Does this suggest that the reincarnational readings are also valid?

We are even willing now to consider the survival of human personality as a worthy subject for scientific investigation—mainly because evidence is piling up that cannot be explained entirely by any other thesis; but reincarnation is still on the outskirts, an unwanted stepchild who keeps returning to plague us. Some excellent men, including Dr. Ian Stevenson of the University of Virginia, are beginning to shed some light here, however, through their own investigations.

It is still scientifically almost impossible to prove that a living personality actually was a person who lived in, say, the seventeenth century, even if the individual could demonstrate beyond doubt personal knowledge beyond normal capacity that in itself was definitely valid. Suppose, for example, that John X came up with information concerning a Bishop Y who was known to have lived in a particular town in the 1700's—information which amazed scholars with its detail. Other explanations besides that of reincarnation could theoretically account for the situation.

In methods unknown to us, the information could have been subconsciously gathered. It could have been received clairvoyantly (as Croiset has given aid to scholars in their examination of old manuscripts); or through communication with the actual personality involved, in a medium-like relationship. Granted all these explanations seem as complicated as reincarnation, they need to be taken into consideration. Specific cases from India would seem to have no other explanation than that reincarnation is a fact, but they are largely ignored in this country, perhaps because the above-mentioned explanations could also serve to explain them.

Apparitions definitely do belong in the field of the parapsychologists, and each such case is carefully studied. There is proof that they do exist, and documented instances are on record in the psychic societies. This is not proof that the personality *as we know it* necessarily survives death, however. It is proof that something of the personality survives, which may be a different thing. Such apparitions are suggestive of the survival of human personality, of this there can be no doubt. We may find it easier to dismiss such instances but this in no way affects the facts involved. Such apparitions are valid whether or not they may prove embarrassing to our present theories, conceptions or misconceptions.

Spiritualism has done much to further ESP investigation, particularly in the past. The atmosphere of confidence and belief has probably helped many in such circles to develop their own abilities. Unfortunately fraud exists in spiritualistic circles as it does anywhere else. The seance atmosphere itself tends to draw the well-meaning, self-deluded individual, as well as serious persons who are more discriminating in what they will accept and not accept.

Every town in this country has its mediums. They operate within spiritualistic circles and on their own. Many are honest and mean well but have little ability. Some have legitimate abilities. Sorely needed are representatives from parapsychology institutes, well-trained in the techniques of investigation, who would seek these people out, encourage them to study and develop their talents, weed out the frauds and persuade the legitimate mediums to let their abilities be investigated.

Obviously money would be needed for such an undertaking, and it is not available. There would also be many difficulties, probably from some of the mediums themselves, from spiritualistic circles and from the parapsychologists who are not set up to handle such extensive investigations at this time. It is a grave error, however, to take it for granted that all these self-styled mediums are frauds or fakes, simply because they have not been studied.

What we would like is to isolate ESP as a biologist isolates a virus, but this is impossible. What we want are predictable experiments, but the human personality is not predictable. ESP seems to operate best when we do not rely upon the physical senses for communication, when we do not use the logical thought processes, when we are not oriented mainly toward immediate physical reality.

These characteristics naturally make investigation of such phenomena difficult. It is my contention however, that the characteristics of ESP can be studied to some extent through an exploration of the human personality as it operates within the dream framework and dissociated states, when it is inner directed.

In the opinion of this writer, the human personality, if it survives the change which we call death, will display in part the same sort of consciousness and behavior as is shown by the living personality when it is dissociated from the ego. Since subconscious language is also part of the whole ESP framework, such an investigation would also serve to aid us in interpreting this inner symbolism.

The way in which the personality works under these conditions should tell us much about the ways in which extrasensory perceptions are received and used. Careful study of precognitive dreams would be invaluable. Those dreams which are not clear cut but are mixed with other subconscious material could perhaps tell us even more about the way the personality uses this information than can more startling precognitive dreams. Psychologists have embarked upon investigations of the dream state, but to my knowledge the dreams are not classified with precognition in mind.

The experiments in this book should have allowed the reader to recognize and use at least some of his own abilities. The prediction experiments in particular should be conducted by all of you who are interested in ESP. There is at least some possibility that these experiments can help to put precognition on some sort of consistent basis. As far as I know this experiment is original with the writer. The Psychological Time experiments were initiated by suggestions given in the Seth Material, although variations have been used by others in the past.

There is no doubt that some dreams are precognitive. The experiments given in this book concerning such dreams have been used, though not extensively, by other investigators, particularly J. W. Dunne. A nationwide acceptance of these dream experiments, conducted by the masses, would be most beneficial, not only in familiarizing the public with precognitive dreams through direct experience, but in strengthening the general case for them. Robert and I have some reason to suspect that you can cause yourself to have such dreams by giving the suggestion that you do so, before falling asleep. We have only begun on this particular part of our own work, so we do not have enough data to allow us to draw any conclusions.

Many of you may find that you possess the abilities necessary for success with the "Ouija" board, automatic writing or automatic speech, though this last is somewhat more unusual. These in themselves are not evidence of any ESP however, but are methods of reaching the subconscious. On occasion they may also be devices that will allow you to recognize and use legitimate ESP abilities. An honest evaluation of the material you receive in these ways will give you a good idea as to whether you are tapping your own subconscious, or whether you are actually tapping other forces beyond the recognized boundaries of the personal self.

There are some good reasons to suppose that hypnotism may allow the individual to use his own extrasensory perceptions by enabling him to switch the focus of his attention from the physical environment to the inner environment. It should be mentioned, however, that hallucinations can be induced under hypnosis through the use of suggestion. A hypnotized subject can be persuaded that a table has jumped eight feet from the floor, and he will swear to it. Obviously this does not mean that the table moved an inch. The hallucination, in such a case, would simply be induced in the subject by the hypnotist. It is possible that suggestion might play some part in mediumistic seances, where physical objects are seen to move about the room in an extraordinary manner. This does not mean that all such effects are caused by suggestion, however. Those of you who are interested in hypnosis should read some of the excellent books dealing with the principles of modern scientific hypnosis.

Self-hypnotism will allow the reader to become acquainted with the trance state, to achieve that dissociated condition of consciousness in which ESP abilities often show themselves. There is nothing unnatural about trance states in general. This writer can say without fear of being contradicted that each reader of this book has been in a trance state without even knowing it many times in his life.

Those of you who feel uncomfortable with self-hypnosis need not use it, however. Alternate ways of increasing concentration and focusing inward have been given. The momentary release of the personality from the dictates of the ego is what we want for these particular experiments. It makes no difference what we call the achieved state of consciousness, or what name we give to the methods used.

Hypnosis leads to heightened inner concentration by shutting out physical distractions. It is not like a sleep state, though it is true that certain general comparisons between sleep and hypnotic trance can be made. If a hypnotist in his induction suggests that the subject feel sleepy or go to sleep, however, the subject will do both. If, on the other hand, the hypnotist does not make such suggestions, the subject will not feel any sleepier than he did a few moments earlier unless—and this is an important point— the subject is already convinced that hypnotic trance is similar to the sleep state.

Hypnosis can be used to induce a sleeplike condition; this does not mean that hypnosis as such must, of necessity, induce a sleeplike condition. It can be used to much advantage to increase consciousness and direct attention, allowing a student to study for a difficult examination, for example. It can also be used as a method of building up self-confidence in a personality and of assuring him that he can use all his abilities. It can be used in the manner we are suggesting in this book—as a way of bypassing egotistical concerns so that ESP can make itself known more easily.

I am only beginning to use my own abilities. It should be remembered that I had no ESP experiences before beginning the experiments listed in this book. My husband has had success with all of the experiments also. His work with daily predictions has been particularly interesting. We have only begun to touch upon some other experiments which cannot be given here because we have not yet devoted sufficient work or time to them.

Is there an astral body, for example? It is thought by many that we possess an intangible inner body, composed of some substance that is between matter and non-matter. Others think that this astral body is electromagnetic. The whole idea originally sounded rather far-fetched to this writer. Yet some of my experiences seem to suggest that astral travel or travel in this astral body is legitimate. Further experimentation may lead to some answers.

As far as the Seth sessions are concerned, they still continue. When this book is in your hands, over 200 sessions will have been held. The Seth voice is heard with increasing frequency. Its volume alone raises an important question. Either Seth is definitely what he says he is and has energy at his command to push my own vocal cords beyond normal limits, or the subconscious has amazing abilities to manipulate physical organisms, far beyond those generally supposed.

The writer has spoken as Seth in a deep, masculine-like voice that literally boomed out for hours, all the while discussing various complicated matters logically and concisely. One such session, taped, was directed to a well-known psychologist, at his request. Because of the volume the voice can achieve, we rarely hold such a session in our apartment, but at the home of friends in the country.

Seth says that he is an energy-personality essence, no longer operating within the physical system. Quite simply, we do not know who or what he is. We have been told unofficially by a psychologist that Seth does not display the usual signs of a secondary personality. The various physical effects and the several instances of clairvoyance shown in the sessions do not prove anything one way or another in that respect.

Despite my own disinclinations concerning physical effects, these may prove important in the future. If Seth appears—and I see him—in full bloom, so to speak, in the middle of our living room, in good light, then I for one will be more than willing to admit that he is indeed what he says he is. Robert has seen several definite changes in my own features during sessions. He and a witness observed, in excellent light, the odd materialization that appeared before my face on the same evening that the witness saw the apparition. I did not see the apparition, however. Since other materializations are infrequent and involve my own person, I have not observed these myself.

Indications do not point toward suggestion as being responsible for these effects, particularly since they happened in good light. Seth recently stated that the feature changes could be photographed and we intend to design some future sessions with this in mind. The voice is hardly a hallucination. Recordings of it are proof of that. The whole affair does not appear to be of subconscious origin, unless we are willing to completely reassess our definitions of the subconscious, and assign to it powers and abilities far beyond those now accorded to it.

Seth himself recently discussed these matters with the earlier mentioned psychologist in one of the most bizarre conversations I have ever been involved in. In the psychologist's office, Seth, Robert, the psychologist and myself carried on a lengthy conversation in which I would be myself, and then Seth, with such rapidity that all of us were astonished.

Regardless of what Seth is or is not, however, the Seth Material constantly intrigues us with its high intellectual content, its logic, psychological insights, psychological and scientific theories. The material deals with the study of the human personality as seen in the waking, dream and trance states, discusses, among other things, the nature of physical matter, the expanding universe theory, anti-matter and the nature of time. Experiments are suggested in many instances. We are not concerned here with a tract of high generalizations, in pseudoscientific or mystic language, which could be rather easily dismissed. When Seth maintains that physical matter is formed subconsciously, he then proceeds to explain exactly how this is done, and then gives very convincing demonstrations to prove his point. He also states that mathematicians can also reach the same conclusion, working from their own bases.

Since some of our most practical theories have come out of the blue—from subconscious or intuitional sources —the ideas presented in the Seth Material should be given serious consideration, regardless of their source or because of it, according to your viewpoint. The material offers the most logical and acceptable theory with which we have come into contact, offering a consistent and original model of the universe that can be accepted regardless of personal religious beliefs; it offers a bridge between science, psychology and parapsychology. It suggests laboratory experiments that can prove the hypothesis presented, and deals extensively with the nature of ESP in general.

Parapsychologists have unfortunately been besieged by numberless manuscripts, some ridiculous in nature, some philosophically "woolly" or vaguely spiritualistic and some plainly obscene, most produced through automatic writing, some through automatic speech. They are understandably reluctant to consider such manuscripts seriously. All material gained in that manner is not of the same caliber, however, and a close investigation of various superior manuscripts might be most useful and productive.

An unfortunate result of the insistence upon the scientific method in the field has been a lack of intelligent theories to explain the definite, observable facts. Yet a theory is needed not only to explain these facts, but to provide a possible framework for further investigations and experiments. Theories are very much a part of the scientific method—though this is too often overlooked. Scientists are continually testing theories, discarding them as new discoveries show them inadequate, and forming new theories to explain current facts. A theory is not necessarily a truth. It is a working explanation to fit the facts at hand. From this standpoint the Seth Material offers an excellent contribution.

The reader of this book will discover for himself,

through the experiments, that he has abilities of which he has been largely ignorant in the past, that extrasensory perception is not unnatural, occult or supernatural. The human personality simply has a greater reality and greater awareness than we have supposed. If apparitions are scientifically proven—and some excellent parapsychologists insist that they have been—then they must be accepted as wholly "natural," existing within the framework of a Nature which we have only begun to explore.

Since beginning the experiments listed in this book, the writer and her husband have had many precognitive dreams, all documented; we have had experiences that cannot be explained except by the admission that the human personality is to some degree independent of physical matter, physical space and time; and we envy the readers who now embark upon these explorations. We look back with wonder at our own initiation into these realities and anticipate further progress.

Since the possibility of an investigation of Seth was mentioned to us by a psychologist, we have begun on our own an informal series of experiments calculated to test Seth's clairvoyant and telepathic abilities, among other things. I mentioned this earlier. Although we have barely begun, so far the results have been rewarding. Seth correctly identified the contents of a sealed envelope which was tossed into my lap during a session. This time I did not know that any test at all was planned. My eyes were closed. The room was well lighted. I merely touched the envelope. Studies with concealed objects are also being planned.

The results have done much to improve my own confidence under test conditions. We cannot know at this time whether these abilities are Seth's or my own. In any case we are only beginning, but it is hoped that the experience will allow me to relax and deal calmly with such an official investigation in case one does occur.

Further experiments, already begun, include telepathic and clairvoyant tests conducted without Seth, by Robert and myself, with both of us at different times acting as subject. It takes considerable time and effort to set up scientific procedures in a regular household, but we do our best to take all necessary precautions against subconscious "cheating." We will have suitable observers when this is necessary.

The Seth Material itself has presented further ideas for future investigations, and we are also embarking upon these. Seth maintains that, with proper preliminary suggestion, the individual can cause himself to have clairvoyant dreams. Other intriguing concepts concerning dream therapy have been given, and we intend to investigate them through experiments suggested by Seth.

A reading list is included at the end of this book. These books will give you an excellent background in the field of ESP and will increase your knowledge and insight. You owe it to yourself to discover exactly what work has been done in the field, what proofs have been achieved, what progress has been made and what progress is needed. These abilities are yours. These investigations therefore concern you, in a most personal way.

In the meantime, begin your own investigation. Do you have the ability to look into the future? My answer is yes. But don't take my word for it. Conduct your own experiments. Find out for yourself. Do you communicate telepathically with friends and relatives? Only your own experience and your own records can adequately give you an answer. The challenge and the rewards are yours.

Inner space will be our next frontier. Never has so much been possible. Never has the individual human personality had such an opportunity to develop his own abilities and to contribute to the knowledge of his race. There are hazards—as with any endeavor. There are setbacks. But the project is more than worth your while. For what we are is only partly contained within physical matter. Free of superstition and ignorance, let us, for the first time in our history as a race, come to grips with the intangible parts of ourselves. Undiscovered man is still to emerge with full knowledge of his potentials. Use of those potentials may yet make us truly wise.

At our last session we asked Seth for a few suitable

comments to be used in concluding this book. I include them here.

Excerpts from Session 180, August 23, 1965

The human personality has no limitations except those which it accepts. There are no limits to its development or growth, if it will accept no limits. There are no boundaries to the self except those boundaries which the self arbitrarily creates and perpetuates. There is no veil through which human perception cannot see, except the veil of ignorance which is pulled down by the materialistic ego.

That which appears empty, such as your space, is empty only for those who do not perceive, who are blind because they fear to perceive that which the ego cannot understand. The ego, however, is also capable of greater knowledge and potentiality and scope. It dwells in the physical universe, but it can indeed also perceive and appreciate other realities. The ego is part of the personality and as such it can partake of sturdier, heartier, more vivid realities. The personality can dwell and does dwell in many worlds at once.

The inquiring intuitions and the searching self, like summer winds, can travel in small and large spaces, can know of actualities that are more minute than pinheads and more massive than galaxies. The power and ability of the human personality, in a most practical manner, can be seen as unlimited.

Suggested Reading List

CAYCE, HUGH LYNN. *Venture Inward.* New York, Evanston and London: Harper and Row, 1964.

DINGWALL, ERIC and LANDON-DAVIES, JOHN. *The Unknown—Is It Nearer?* New York: New American Library, 1956.

DOYLE, ARTHUR CONAN. *History of Spiritualism.* New York: George H. Doran Co., 1926.

ESTABROOKS, G. H. *Spiritism.* New York: E. P. Dutton & Co., Inc., 1947.

FEILDING, EVERARD. *Sittings With Eusapia Palladino and Other Studies.* New Hyde Park, N. Y.: University Books, Inc., 1963.

HEYWOOD, ROSALIND. *Beyond the Reach of Sense.* New York: E. P. Dutton & Co., Inc., 1961.

LeCRON, LESLIE. *Self Hypnotism.* Englewood Cliffs, N. J.: Prentice Hall, Inc., 1964.

MILLER, R. DeWITT. *Impossible Yet It Happened.* New York: Ace Books, Inc., 1947.

MURPHY, GARDNER. *Challenge of Psychical Research.* New York: Harper & Bros., 1961.

MYERS, F. W. H. *Human Personality and Its Survival of Bodily Death.* New York: Green & Co., 1915.

POLLACK, JACK HARRISON. *Croiset the Clairvoyant.* New York: Bantam, 1965.

PRINCE, WALTER FRANKLIN. *The Case of Patience Worth.* New Hyde Park, N. Y.: University Books, Inc., 1964.

RHINE, J. B. *New World of the Mind.* New York: William Sloane Associates, Inc., 1953.

RHINE, J.B. *New Frontiers of the Mind.* New York: Farrar & Rinehart, 1937.

SMITH, SUSY. *World of the Strange*. New York: Pyramid
Publications, Inc., 1963.

STEARN, JESS. *The Door to the Future*. Garden City,
N. Y.: Doubleday & Co., Inc., 1963.

SUGRUE, THOMAS. *There Is A River*. New York: Holt &
Co., 1942.

The following are also suggested:

Journals from these foundations:
Parapsychology Laboratory, College Station, Durham,
N.C.
American Society for Psychical Research, Inc., 880
Fifth Avenue, New York, N.Y. 10021
Parapsychology Foundation, Inc., 29 West 57 Street,
New York, N.Y. 10019
Fate Magazine
Tomorrow Magazine

"*Imagine waking up to find yourself over 40 and overweight!*"

...EILEEN FORD, *Head of the world's largest model agency.*

"*It was downright embarrassing. I gave myself 3 weeks to make a comeback and...*

lost 16 pounds plus 5 inches."

NOW step-by-step and day-by-day she reveals to you her own beautifying plan in her new book, *Eileen Ford's A More Beautiful You in 21 Days.* The plan uses everything she knows about—

EXERCISE—not boring and repetitive, but a pleasant, varied program that you can do in a few minutes.

DIET—delicious, slimming menus and recipes for 21 days for you and your family from the world's best restaurants.

BEAUTY CARE—How to cure The Frizzies. First aid and lasting beauty for fingernails and hands. Quick make-up magic. The secret to a sexy voice. How to make the most of your assets. And many, many more.

You have nothing to lose but inches and years!

At your bookstore or mail this coupon now for free 10-day trial

---

SIMON AND SCHUSTER, Dept. 61, 630 Fifth Ave., N.Y. 10020
Please send my copy of *Eileen Ford's A More Beautiful You in 21 Days.* If I'm not convinced that it can help me, I may return it within 10 days and owe nothing. Otherwise, I will send $9.95 plus mailing as payment in full.

(Please Print)

Name_____

Address_____

City_____ State_____ Zip_____

☐ SAVE POSTAGE. Check here if you enclose check or money order for the books you want—then we pay postage. 10-day trial privilege guarantee holds.

☐ Also please send "*Eileen Ford's Book of Model Beauty,*" at $9.95. Money back guarantee if not delighted.

S75/3A

How to stay healthy all the time.

> *"I can recommend this book for authoritative answers to questions that continually come up about health and how to live."*—Harry J. Johnson, M.D., Chairman, Medical Board Director, Life Extension Institute.

Wouldn't it be wonderful if your whole family could stay healthy all the time?

It may now be possible, thanks to PREVENTIVE MEDICINE. This is the modern approach to health care. Its goal is to prevent illness before it even has a chance to strike!

A new book called **THE FAMILY BOOK OF PREVENTIVE MEDICINE** shows how you can take advantage of this preventive approach, and make it an everyday reality for yourself and your family. More than 700 pages long—and written in clear, simple language.

TELLS YOU ALL ABOUT THE LATEST MEDICAL ADVANCES

For example, the new knowledge of risk factors in disease is a vital tool of preventive medicine. With it, your doctor might pinpoint you as, say, a high heart attack risk *long before your heart actually gives you any trouble.* He could then prescribe certain changes in your diet and habits—perhaps very minor ones—that could remove the danger entirely. This would be preventive medicine at its ideal best! But even if a disease has already taken root, new diagnostic techniques can reveal its presence earlier than ever before. And, as a rule, the sooner a disease is discovered, the more easily it is cured.

SEND NO MONEY—10 DAYS' FREE EXAMINATION

Mail the coupon below, and **THE FAMILY BOOK OF PREVENTIVE MEDICINE** will be sent to you for free examination. Then, if you are not convinced that it can help you protect the health of your entire family, return it within 10 days and owe nothing. Otherwise, we will bill you for $12.95 plus mailing costs. At all bookstores, or write to Simon and Schuster, Dept. S-53, 630 Fifth Ave., New York, N.Y. 10020.

SIMON AND SCHUSTER, Dept. S-53
630 Fifth Ave., New York, N.Y. 10020

Please send me on approval a copy of THE FAMILY BOOK OF PREVENTIVE MEDICINE. If not convinced that this book belongs permanently in my home, I may return it within 10 days and owe nothing. Otherwise, you will bill me for $12.95, plus mailing costs.

Name..

Address...

City..State..............Zip..........

☐ SAVE. Enclose $12.95 now, and publisher pays mailing costs. Same 10-day return privilege with full refund guaranteed. (New York residents please add applicable sales tax.)

P 65/2